The Romance of **Firefighting**

L. Maurer.

THE AMERICAN FIREMAN,

Prompt to the Rescue.

The Romance of

Firefighting

by

R O B E R T   S .   H O L Z M A N

ILLUSTRATED

BONANZA BOOKS   •   NEW YORK

THE ROMANCE OF FIREFIGHTING

0-517-001969
Copyright © MCMLVI by Robert S. Holzman
Library Of Congress Catalog Card Number: 56-8752
All rights reserved.
This edition is published by Bonanza Books
a division of Crown Publishers, Inc.
by arrangement with Harper & Row, Publishers.
d e f g h
Manufactured in the United States Of America

To the memory of

MY FATHER

a lifelong buff

(here photographed with Rex II, F.D.N.Y.)

Contents

The Romance of **Firefighting**

Factory Fire On September 19, 1874 occurred this catastrophic fire in a granite mill in Fall River, Massachusetts. As so frequently is the case, panic rather than the flames is responsible for most of the loss of life.

The Romance Never Went Away

"The sons of all the gentlemen here are volunteer engineers and firemen, and great is the delight they take in tearing up and down the street, accompanied by red lights, speaking trumpets, and a rushing, roaring escort of running amateur extinguishers, who make night hideous with their bawling and bellowing." But these words of the celebrated actress Fanny Kemble, penned in New York in 1832, are apt to convey a highly erroneous impression. All volunteer firemen were *not* gentlemen's sons. Many a smoke-eater would have resented a hint that he was anything but one of the boys.

Who were the first volunteer firemen? They were the leading citizens in the community, and they were the nobodies. They were the wealthy merchants, and they were the lowly clerks. They were actors, retired soldiers, butchers, shipbuilders, victualers, street brawlers without visible means of support. In short, they were a cross section of America.

What did the volunteer firemen get for their pains, loss of time, and inconvenience? Usually the firemen received exemption from jury and military duty after ten years' service. But public duty usually was the lodestar. There was prestige in belonging to certain companies. There was satisfaction in work well done. And there was the thrill of being a volunteer fireman.

Once he was wearing his red shirt and black helmet, the volunteer fireman knew no peers. Here (as almost nowhere else) was real democracy. The bookkeeper grappled a tow rope next to the banker, and at the firehouse socials anyone could introduce his wife to the alderman. There was the leavening influence of common danger. There was a wonderful *esprit de corps*.

If the fireman was insignificant when he was alone, he was one of the lords of creation when he was with the boys. Traffic was stopped, municipal life was diverted, the medieval elements of fire and water were subjugated. Local governments trembled before the mighty political force that was the volunteer firemen collectively.

The firemen were proudly conscious of their importance in the community. Yet no man considered himself to be a member of the community's fire department, for there *was* none. There was merely a collection of fire companies. Each man strove mightily to make *his* company the best one in town. That meant humbling the other companies: in racing to a conflagration, in getting a stream on the blaze, in amount of water pumped, in appearance of the fire apparatus. At first this was a friendly rivalry, such as stimulates endeavor in any field. But in time the competition became fierce. The men spent more energy in battling with other companies, in many instances, than they did in fighting fires. Brawlers and toughs were recruited, not because they were good firemen, but because they could wield a mighty bludgeon. Public service, the reason for being a volunteer fireman, was impaired. That was one of the causes for the ending of the regime of the volunteers in the larger communities.

But there were other reasons. As communities

CAUGHT IN THE CANVAS HELD BY CITIZENS.

ESCAPING BY MEANS OF BLANKETS.

RESCUE OF WOMEN BY FIREMEN OF HOOK AND LADDER TRUCKS NOS. 1 AND 2.

CLINGING TO THE WINDOW-SILLS.

AT THE MORGUE.

The Great Milwaukee Fire   Here are some episodes at the Milwaukee fire of '92.

grew, the protection problem became greater. Buildings were taller, more closely congregated. More powerful engines were needed to cope with fires. Steamers were developed to deal with the problem. At first the volunteers refused to have anything to do with steam fire engines; the men insisted that they were sturdy Americans and not mechanics. They fiercely loved their hand apparatus, kissed it fondly after victories over rival companies, and bedecked it with beautiful embellishments. But the steam age irresistibly took over. Small professional, well-trained departments assumed the work on a full-time basis. The day of the volunteer was over in the cities.

The volunteer fireman left his mark in many places. Songs were written for him, plays were written around him. Stately clipper used him as a figurehead. Of the innumerable subjects for illustration, Currier & Ives found firemen to be about the most popular for their lithographs. Unusually courageous regiments were recruited exclusively from the volunteer firemen (as the Ellsworth and the Hawkins Fire Zouaves in the Civil War). Many mayors and other public figures attained their first notice through service as volunteer firemen. And never was there a more courageous, hard-working, self-sacrificing, colorful group of citizens than the "vamps."

The advent of the paid fire departments took place in the larger communities in the 1850's and 1860's. Yet that did not signify the knell of the romantic age of fire fighting. Few volunteer firemen would relinquish their posts of honor at the tow lines to horses, but the paid departments, ever efficiency-conscious, had no such sentimental attachment to pulling the "injines." Besides, the need for heavier engines and the traversing of greater distances urgently dictated that horses be used for

Din   Foremen of rival companies are hollering their men to greater efforts; but the chief engineer in the center, because of his greater experience, can probably out-bellow both of them in this Thomas & Wylie lithograph. *Library of Congress*

A Baltimore Theatre Fire This Geo. C. Warner lithograph shows the burning of the Front Street Theatre and Circus on February 3, 1938. Note the extra shifts of firemen who are ready to take their places at the "brakes" when the men now pumping become exhausted. The uniforms are similar to those then worn by Philadelphia firemen. *The Peale Museum, Baltimore*

pulling fire vehicles. For another half century, the streets clattered beneath the steel hooves of gallant fire horses, who seemed even more magnificent when pulling a smoke-belching nickel steamer or a lengthy ladder truck. The love that the volunteer firemen had had for their fragile engines was even surpassed by the love that the paid firemen had for their superb fire horses, which were living, responsive, pathetically eager to do their duty under any conditions. The age of romance was continuing in wondrous form.

Then at different times beginning in the first decade of the twentieth century, the Industrial Revolution was completed in the fire departments.

An Early Pumper This old illustration shows a fire scene in New York in about 1730. The men are using an engine with side pump-handles. How even this feeble stream could come from a pumper served by so few men is incomprehensible. Down the street another engine is coming to render needed assistance.

The "Lawrence" Here is an 1859 drawing of a Boston steamer. Note the fuel-carrying cart attached to the rear wheels of the pumper.

Milwaukee Street Scene (*Above*) This turn of the century photograph shows a hook and ladder truck jouncing along a dirt surfaced road en route to a fire. The driver is strapped to his seat by a forerunner of today's safety belt. *The Milwaukee Journal*

Leaving Quarters (*Below*) Hook & Ladder Company #68 of the Brooklyn Fire Department is just leaving its station at fire headquarters. On this early type of extension truck, the tillerman was obliged to sit in very cramped space beneath the main ladder. Note the size of these horses. *Ed Waterman*

A Worker in Rochester Snow acts as background at this fire in Rochester, N.Y., on a winter's day. Water from the hose lines has covered the buildings with ice. Falling walls have kept the men at a respectable distance, which would be forgotten if a rescue were to be made. *Ed Waterman*

the horse. Since there was now a propelling engine, even the colorful steamer was doomed. Machinery had taken the place of man and animal. Gasoline was king of the streets.

We cannot turn back the clock even if we would. The techniques of the volunteers were sufficient unto their day but not unto ours. Yet we look back at their glorious deeds with more than a nostalgic eye. We look back with awe, with reverence and admiration. Present-day firemen are as brave as their prototypes of the past, and men and equipment are infinitely more efficient; but to many persons, the romantic age of fire fighting is gone.

Such a belief is illusory. It was not a red shirt or a puffing steamer that made the old-time fireman a romantic figure. The romantic aura arose from the nature of the age-old struggle between Man and Fire; and the adoption of spray nozzles, smoke ejectors, and foam chemicals does not change the true nature of this heroic battle. Today's fireman is just as necessary and vital as were his forerunners. Automation can never make the fireman obsolete. "If Prometheus was worthy of the wrath of Heaven for kindling the first fire upon earth, how ought all the gods to honor the men who make it their professional business to put it out."

"Get Out!" This scene, however frequently witnessed, never ceased to be exciting. The fire alarm telegraph has sounded a box number to which this company responds, and the house watchman bellowed a loud, "Get out!" Then he rushed to snap on the mechanical collars of the horses, which already have taken their places beneath harnesses suspended from the ceiling. To the rear, the horses assigned to the hose cart also may be seen in place. An instant later and the apparatus will be in the street, while the men finish their dressing. Only the crown above the smoke stack will still be seen, dangling from a wire attached to the ceiling.

A Modern Pumper with Searchlights American-LaFrance-Foamite Corporation

10

"Throw Out Your Buckets!"

Leather Fire Buckets Here are two examples of the bucket that was for so long the chief fire fighting apparatus of the land. *Smithsonian Institute*

Although each community had its own peculiarities, there was a general similarity in the development of fire fighting in the American colonies. At first, leather fire buckets were purchased, and a few men were assigned to keeping this simple equipment in order. Next, each householder was required to supply a certain quota of buckets, to be used in a community sense. Certain precautionary measures were decreed by proper authority, such as the banning of wooden chimneys and thatched roofs; perhaps a system of fines for violators was used to finance the cost of additional equipment. Then the community purchased equipment such as ladders and hooks, the cost frequently being secured by means of a tax on chimneys or hearths, the two most common causes of the fires that this equipment would be used to fight. In time, a bucket brigade might be organized to respond to fires with an efficiency that on-the-scene recruits could not match. The most prominent members of

a community made a point of volunteering for fire duty, to set a good example for their less public-spirited compatriots. As communities became larger and wealthier, a fire engine might be imported, generally from England. By the time that a second fire company was organized, a sense of keen rivalry between the companies would exist. The day of exuberant, overly eager firemen had arrived.

American fire protection may be said to have been started by Peter Stuyvesant, the doughty one-legged Dutch governor of New Amsterdam. On November 14, 1647, he requested his advisers to counsel him on regulations for fires, "which might break out here as well as in other places. It must be done with the least expense and danger to the community." In 1648, fire wardens were appointed by him; wooden chimneys were forbidden, on pain of penalties; and householders were fined twenty-five florins if fires occurred in their homes. The fines were used to purchase buckets, hooks, and

North Carolina's First Engine This apparatus dates back to 1765. Unlike most fire engines, this one had to be carried by handles to the scene of the fire. The leather buckets are for filling the water chamber. *Hall of History, North Carolina Department of Archives and History*

Fireman George Washington   Washington was an enthusiastic fireman.
He belonged to the Friendship Company of Alexandria, Virginia, which had been formed
in about 1775. He purchased this machine for his company from Gibbs of Philadelphia.
Insurance Company of North America

A New York Bucket Brigade   This oil painting on cardboard by William
P. Chappel, made in about 1809, shows a bucket brigade passing containers of water
from a pump to a fire engine, whence a stream is being directed by a hose line. On the
left, a man familiar with the effectiveness of fire fighting techniques of that day is pru-
dently wetting down the roof of his building. *The Edward W. C. Arnold Collection, Metropolitan Museum of Art. Photograph Courtesy The Museum of The City of New York.*

Primitive Fire Engine This picture of a fire in about 1733 shows a pumper that is operated by weight as well as muscle, in the manner of a railroad flat-car. The building, fortunately, has stone walls which should keep the fire from spreading.

ladders. Later that year, wardens were authorized to visit every house in order to see that the regulations were being complied with faithfully. By the ordinance of December 15, 1657, Stuyvesant ordered changes made in the construction of chimneys and roofs, and dangerous hayricks were forbidden. A tax of one beaver or eight florins was imposed upon every house in order to get money for the purchase of leather buckets. In 1658, the first American firemen, the Prowlers, were designated: eight men with buckets and ladders patrolled the streets of New Amsterdam from nightfall until the morning drumbeat.

Boston, as one of the leading communities in the New World, took its fire prevention activities seriously. After a serious conflagration in 1653, each householder was required to procure a ladder "that shall rech to the ridg of the house" and a "pole of about 12 feet long, with a large swob at the end of it, to rech the rofe . . . to quench fire in case of such danger." In 1679, the town imported a fire engine from England, and a carpenter with assistants was named to service the pumper. This was twenty years before lordly Paris acquired its first fire engine. (But Boston did not acquire another engine until 1704.)

Philadelphia recognized quite quickly that chimneys were the source of most local fires. Yet William Penn earlier had spoken of "a great country town built for the promotion of health and comfort, and free from the dangers of fire." So in 1696, the City of Brotherly Love decreed that any householder who cleaned his chimney by firing it would be fined. There was a heavy forty-shilling fine if a chimney caught fire by reason of its not having been cleaned properly, the money to be used to purchase leather fire buckets.

The first specialized equipment in America for fighting fires was the leather fire bucket, usually of three gallons' capacity. In the better-organized communities, a watchman would give the alarm of fire and then he would bellow, "Throw out your buckets!" Householders tossed their leather buckets into the street, and those persons rushing to the fire would pick up these receptacles. Any person who happened to be at the scene of fire was required to do duty, for the duration. Two human lines were then formed between the burning structure and the nearest source of water: one line was used to pass the full buckets of water up to the blaze, while the other line was used to return the empties to the well, pump, or river. If anyone was so foolhardy as to attempt to cross a bucket line, he would be doused with water; the fire could wait. After the flames were subdued (or the building had burned down), the buckets were piled in front of the city hall or meeting house, and each householder would call for his bucket, which was generally emblazoned with his name, initials, or (occasionally) coat of arms. Some communities provided poles, so that two men could carry, stretcher-fashion, twelve buckets on each pole.

Various methods of obtaining buckets were in vogue. Some communities supplied the buckets, which were financed by fines or by a special fire tax. Other localities required that buckets be supplied in accordance with some formula: one bucket per house, per chimney, or per hearth. Business establishments had to provide buckets in accordance with the hazardous nature of the activity conducted there. Thus a bakehouse might have to supply four buckets, while brewhouses might have to supply nine.

Fire engines (other than those of antiquity) are believed to have been invented in Germany, but the early American apparatus was imported from England. Apparently the first engine to be built in the colonies was a machine that Abraham Bickley sold to Philadelphia for fifty pounds in 1718. Throughout most of the eighteenth century, however, colonial engines were generally English-made, the Richard Newsham pumpers being preferred.

A Newsham Pumper in Action This fire scene appeared on the engraved policy head of the Mutual Assurance Company of Virginia. *Colonial Williamsburg*

The Newsham engine, which was patented in 1725, was the first pumper to throw a continuous stream. Earlier engines had been merely a sucking pump and forcing pump combined, which projected water only in spurts and with continuous interruptions. The Newsham pumper had a double-cylinder engine, with an air chamber, gooseneck noozle, and suction pipe. Water was pumped by manually operated brakes; on some models, men stood on the box and threw their weight upon treadles on the pump levers.

Some of the early engines were purchased by public subscription, as was the case with Philadelphia's first three Newsham pumpers in 1730. Newport, in the Rhode Island Colony, formed a fire club in 1726 to purchase an engine.

The first volunteer fire company in the colonies was formed in Philadelphia in 1736 upon the recommendation of Benjamin Franklin. The men of this company, the "Union," furnished their own

equipment. By 1752, Philadelphia had six companies, comprising 225 men, 8 engines, 1,055 buckets, and 36 ladders.

Fire fighting was unusually hazardous in the early days. There were no building codes or safety regulations. The engines pumped so feebly that firemen virtually had to stand on top of the flames to quench them. Water supply was so uncertain that the men never knew when they would be deprived of their weapons. And because of primitive systems of communications, most fires were virtually out of control before the firemen received the alarm. Yet the fire danger was so real that men had to be prepared for duty at any moment. As a result, every able-bodied man was a potential fireman.

The organization of colonial fire departments varied greatly. Where the community did not provide fire equipment, every person helped his unfortunate neighbor, who might have to help him

A Philadelphia-Built Pumper
Richard Mason of Philadelphia built this fire engine (his 117th) in 1792. It was he who introduced end-levers on pumping engine. *Insurance Company of North America*

16

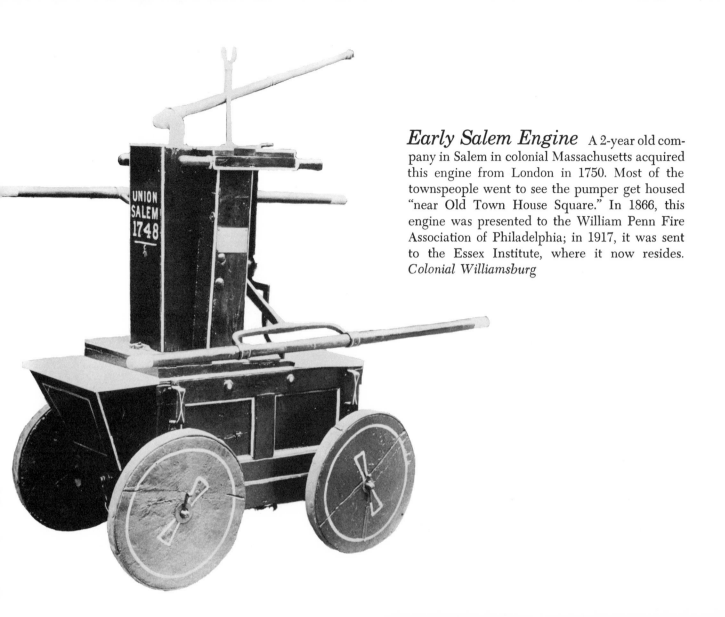

Early Salem Engine A 2-year old company in Salem in colonial Massachusetts acquired this engine from London in 1750. Most of the townspeople went to see the pumper get housed "near Old Town House Square." In 1866, this engine was presented to the William Penn Fire Association of Philadelphia; in 1917, it was sent to the Essex Institute, where it now resides. *Colonial Williamsburg*

the following night. But where fire companies were established by "members," the services of such groups generally were available only to members, unless some desperate householder was able to bribe a company to provide its assistance. There were fire companies that financed themselves solely by the bounty of grateful persons. Other groups were financed by the fire insurance companies, and any uninsured building was allowed to burn down, as a warning to other people not to let their insurance lapse.

In time, the volunteer fire department organization achieved a certain uniformity. Each company was an autonomous body, which elected its own officers and selected its own members. Sometimes a community supplied the equipment; in other

Benjamin Franklin, Fireman Franklin was the chief of the Union Fire Company of Philadelphia, which was claimed to have been the first volunteer fire company in the American colonies. The portrait was painted for the fire company in about 1795. *United Press Photo*

New York in War-Time The great conflagration of 1776 is here shown in a
line engraving by Andre Basset, a Parisian craftsman of that time. He accepted the
British version that Americans had set the fires; one brand-holding rascal has been ap-
prehended by British soldiers in this picture. *Library of Congress*

instances, public subscription took care of finances,
or the company itself provided its apparatus. Discipline was customarily at a company level: that
is, the community had little to say about conduct,
noise, careless use of water or axes, and the like.
Where several companies existed in a community,
a chief engineer was frequently elected by the
firemen, but his actual amount of authority was
uncertain.

The chief characteristic of the American colo-
nists was a desire for freedom, and fire department
organization could not be permitted to interfere
with this freedom. On the other hand, changing
times and conditions usually dictate compromise.
But efficiency was not the only factor to be considered. How could fires be extinguished without loss
of American individuality? How could fire departments function without the authoritarian manner
and quasi-militaristic character of European fire
brigades? How could men function amidst hazardous conditions in a democracy, where there
were no "superiors" to give peremptory orders?
The result was the volunteer fire department which
for many generations was the glory of American
day-by-day life. Just as the successful soldiers of

the American Revolution were private persons who
seized muskets when an enemy threatened, so did
private persons seize tow lines and nozzles and
ladders when fire broke out. Instead of a standing
army, America had a militia of citizens. And the
same principle prevailed in fire fighting for a long,
long time.

NEW YORK'S FIRST "GREAT FIRE"

When General Washington was defeated at the
Battle of Long Island on August 27, 1776, he realized that he would not be able to hold New York
City. On September 2, he wrote to the Continental
Congress to ask whether the city should be destroyed by his departing troops or whether the
place should be left as winter quarters for the
British. "They would derive great convenience
from it on the one hand; and much property
would be destroyed on the other." The American
General Greene strongly urged a scorched earth
policy of not leaving anything behind that the
enemy could use, and Washington was believed
to have shared this opinion, as two-thirds of New
York's property belonged to British loyalists. But
Congress, thinking that the city could be recap-

Early Philadelphia Engine This "gooseneck" pumper was built in 1735. One man could have pulled it. *Philadelphia Museum of Art*

tured by the Americans, refused to grant permission for its destruction.

It was not until September 15 that Washington's army actually left New York. Five days later, a great midnight fire broke out in the semideserted city. The fire raged virtually without check, and large portions of the city were destroyed. Most of the last remnants of the old Dutch occupation were wiped out when the New Amsterdam portion of the community fell to the flames.

The captain of a ship in the harbor reported: "Running upon the deck we could perceive a light, which at the distance we were from it (four miles) was apparently of the size of the flame of a candle. . . . If we could have divested ourselves of the knowledge that it was the property of our fellow-citizens which was consuming, the view might have been esteemed sublime, if not pleasing. The deck of our ship, for many hours, was lighted as if at noonday."

An Imaginative Foreign Artist This wood-cut of New York's Great Fire of 1835 was made by an unknown artist. The view from Coenties Slip appears to have been faithfully reproduced, but the artist clearly had never seen an American fireman of that (or any other) day. The helmets depicted are of a type worn on the European continent and in England, but American smoke-eaters never took to this quasi-military head-gear. *National Board of Fire Underwriters*

A Hospital-Owned Fire Engine The early fire engines in American communities were generally the property of fire companies. Occasionally the apparatus belonged to a community or to a fire insurance company. But this particular pumper was acquired in the first quarter of the nineteenth century by the Pennsylvania Hospital in Philadelphia for its own use. The nation's first hospital (founded by Benjamin Franklin in 1751) wanted to be *sure* that if fire broke out, there would be an engine right on the premises. And that engine is still there today. *Pennsylvania Hospital*

It never has been established which side had set the fire. Americans declared that it was wanton destruction·of a helpless enemy city by the British, who replied that they had found Americans with torches in their hands. A British loyalist minister said that American responsibility was established by the fact that fire bells had been carried away "to prevent notice being given of the destruction they meditated against the city."

One thousand of the 4,200 houses in this city of 30,000 persons were destroyed. Wrote an eyewitness: "The ruins of the southeast side of the town were converted into dwelling places by using the chimneys and parts of the walls which were firm,

and adding spars with old canvas from the ships." This was known locally as Canvas Town.

On land, the War of 1812 went very disastrously for the United States forces. A detachment of British troops landed for a march against the capital, and by August 22, 1814, most families and businesses had fled from Washington. Specie was removed from the banks. On August 24, President Madison and his wife left the city by different roads; they met again at Georgetown. By this time, 99 per cent of Washington's population had left. The last remaining troops retreated eighteen miles to a place of greater safety, after having destroyed the navy yard.

Unopposed, the English soldiers entered Washington. A detachment of one hundred redcoats set fire to the capitol, the presidential mansion, the treasury department, and the war department. The post office building was spared, in deference to the plea that it was a sort of museum of the arts.

Few of the six thousand British troops were engaged in this fire-setting, which took place without hindrance. A patriotic American exclaimed to the British commander, Admiral Cockburn, "If Washington were alive, you could not have done this." "No," replied the invader, "we should not have been at war, nor would *he* have left his capital defenseless for the purpose of making conquests abroad."

The burning of Washington was quite justified, according to the London *Times* of October 6. "It was not occupied with a view to hold it as a military post; still less as the seat of a civil administration; but there are two objects to be attained by its occupation—the destruction of a most formidable naval arsenal belonging to the enemy, and a retribution which should have the effect of stopping the barbarities authorized and encouraged by the American Government. With these views, our forces destroyed the Dockyard with its stores and store-houses; and they also burnt the yet unfinished public edifices of a capital which is at present little more than traced out in the wilds of America. . . . The palace, indeed, so unworthily occupied by a political impostor, was destroyed; and he was rendered ridiculous in the eyes of his fellow-citizens by being driven from the fancied security of the seat of government, at the moment when he was indulging the most gigantic dreams of distant conquest."

The next time that a president of the United States evacuated the White House was on June 15, 1955, when President Eisenhower participated in a nation-wide air raid drill.

The Burning of Washington
This drawing by Beale shows the British troops in the act of firing the Capitol in Washington in 1814. Note the torch-bearing soldiers, both on horseback and on foot. *The Bettmann Archive*

THE AMERICAN FIREMAN,
Facing the Enemy.

Facing the Enemy This Currier & Ives lithograph in "The American Fireman" series was made in 1858. *National Board of Fire Underwriters*

"The Glory of Civilized Life"

"Volunteers in the service of beneficiaries are the glory of civilized life," declared Alexander Townsend in an address to the Charitable Fire Society of Boston in 1809. Certainly the volunteer firemen were one of the glories of the United States for many years, and many European visitors enthusiastically reported the deeds of the smoke-eaters. Shortcomings were noted, but they did not diminish the splendor of the firemen.

In the last decade of the eighteenth century, Moreau de St. Mery thus reported of his voyage to America: "The zeal and eagerness with which all Americans fight fires are admirable, but at the same time there are so many willing helpers and there is so little order that they do more harm than good. . . . It is noticeable that in general the workers have too good a time, that the buckets are left in the streets after the fire, and that hoodlums amuse themselves with them."

The actress Fanny Kemble wrote in further wonderment that Americans didn't even seem to be disturbed by fires. "Perhaps one reason for the perfect coolness with which a fire is endured in New York," she noted in 1835, "is the dexterity and courage of the firemen."

Lady Emmeline Stuart Wortley recorded her enthusiasm in a book published in 1851: "Nowhere,

on the earth, I should think, are such numerous and splendid bodies of firemen; and in no place under the sun, or moon, I honestly think, have they such extensive, incessant, and unlimited practice. And what men in the world ought to make such admirable warriors as firemen? At all times, but especially at the dead hour of midnight, forced to leave their homes at a moment's notice, to start

Rushing to the Conflict Currier & Ives produced this lithograph in their series "The American Fireman" in 1858. *National Board of Fire Underwriters*

THE GREAT FIRE.

We present to our readers, in our extra, issued this day, at 1 o'clock, not only a description, but a GRAPHIC SKETCH of the dreadful fire which last night created so much devastation. We reached the scene about 9 o'clock, this morning—drew a hasty picture of it, and, by 12 o'clock, Johnson, the artist, had the above representation ready for the press. So much for enterprize!

SECOND EDITION.

SATURDAY, 12. M

AWFUL CONFLAGRATION:

DESTRUCTION OF MORE THAN 47 BUILDINGS—AND A GREATER LOSS OF PROPERTY THAN HAS FALLEN UPON PHILADELPHIA BY A SIMILAR CALAMITY FOR MANY YEARS!! WITH LOSS OF LIFE TO THREE FIREMEN!!!

Philadelphia was visited last night and this morning with one of the most disastrous fires that has fallen upon us, for perhaps the last twenty years, attendant with the loss of life to at least two daring firemen! At half past eleven the alarm was given that Mr. Prescott's large provision store, No. 19 South Wharves, between Market & Chesnut sts. was on fire, which within ten or fifteen minutes the building was a solid sheet of flames, from groundfloor to far above the roof. The fire broke out in the immediate vicinity of the wharf and shipping, which a strong high wind from North East carried into the city, saving the shipping, but dealing almost entire destruction to the whole blocks of stores and houses from the wharf to water, and from Water to Front streets.

From Prescott's store, the fire extended to the adjoining building, occupied by C. Cheseborough, G. A. Wood, Wm. J. Stroup, and others, which it burnt entirely out, with nearly all their contents. The books of Mr. Prescott were saved through the daring of Robert Russell, a member of the Hope Hose Co., Bernard, a member of the same company, in attempting to preserve them, previously, was most severely burnt on his face and hands. Jacob Kugler, was also singed in the same attempt. The fire then spread to the store occupied by Newlin & Allibone, Joshua Emlen, and A. W. Jones & Brother, which it also destroyed—Their papers, we believe, were saved.

The fire then extended to Front street, and burnt out the inside of the stores occupied by William R. Thompson & Co., 41 South Front street; John Mee, No. 39 do; J. D. Mifflin, F. G. Smith, agent of the Ulster Iron Company's warehouse, and also agent for Dupont's powder; Davis's suspender factory; John Lloyd's snuff store, Anthony Egan's tavern D. Lahey's tavern.

From the above it communicated to No. 51 Front st., adjoining the above tavern, but the store of S.C. Benting, at the corner of Front and Chesnut was saved. The adjoining building above, on Front st. occupied by James Lourhead, tailor, was burned.

Along the wharf, the fire also extended to C. King & Co's store, No. 19; Geo. Neale's tavern; Adam Hinkle's chandlery; Newbold & Haverstick's counting house, in the second story; Snober & Bunting's store, and Snober and Johnson's warehouse, at the corner of Chesnut street and the wharf, formerly used by the Baltimore Steamboat Company.

At the corner of Water and Chesnut streets, the Fulton house, occupied by Mr. Myers, was destroyed, as was also the warehouses of White, Stevens & Co and John Harding, r., above the hotel on Water street.

The roof of the store on the west side of Front street opposite the fire, occupied by Geo. W. Richards and John Oakman, was burned entirely off by falling sparks, and several other buildings in the neighborhood were more or less injured.

The office of our neighbours of the Pennsylvanian was greatly endangered, requiring the strictest vigilance of those employed there during the entire night, who were several times called upon to extinguish the burning roof.

The number of buildings entirely destroyed, the walls of many of them having fallen in, we have ascertained to be FORTY-SEVEN—and several others have sustained injury nearly equivalent to destruction. They were located as near as we could ascertain as follows:

On Front street below Chesnut, 4; above Chesnut, 10, and two partially injured.

On Water street, above Chesnut, lower side, 9; upper side, 8; two slightly injured.

On Water street, below Chesnut, upper side, 2; lower side, 2.

On Chesnut street, below Front, upper side, 3, and the large Steamboat Coffee House on the lower side, kept by Thos. D. O'Conner.

A double store-house, Taylor's alley, partly occupied as a foreign wine and liquor store, by Mr. J. Rowland, and partly by Mr. Gratz, grocer, and used for storing oil, &c. was completely riddled. This building was adjoining the large drug store of Mr. N. Lennig, which was destroyed by fire in 1836.

A large store-house, No. 35 Front street, above Chesnut, running through to Water street, being fire-proof, was standing uninjured.

We have been enabled with all our enquiries, so dense was the crowd about the smouldering ruins, to gather but few of the particulars in connection with the falling walls at the south-west corner of Chesnut and Water street, which buried beneath it several human beings.

Wm. Maullin, a member of the Good-Will Fire Company, has been taken out dead; and one or two others, attached to the same company, missing, and supposed to have shared a similar fate.

A member of the Hope Hose Company, was dug out of the cellar of the same building, uninjured.

The tailoring establishment of Enoch Allen, at the corner of Chesnut and Water, and the adjoining one below were also burned.

Repeated explosions of gunpowder or saltpetre were heard among the burning ruins. The wind, we repeat, was strong, right upon the city, which, with the narrowness of Water street, enabled the firemen, though they never evinced more alacrity or daring energy, to save little or no property. About one half of the square between Market and Chesnut is injured or destroyed by the fire.

The Camden and Amboy Rail Road office, at the foot of Chesnut street, was saved as if by a miracle. It was a low building, with old wooden roof, and was burned up to by the fire; how it escaped destruction we cannot divine. A contemporary who witnessed the scene says—"the showers of sparks, which fell on the shingle roofs of scores of houses in the vicinity, threatened the whole neighbourhood with danger and destruction. But the firemen exerted themselves with the most becoming and manly spirit. They risked life and limb, and at every moment floated in fear of some disaster. We saw hundreds of them in the most perilous situations, on roofs, walls and chimnies, with buckets and hose pipes, extinguishing the flames as fast as they appeared. Around the flaming edifices—near which the heat was so intense that it was difficult to remain in—they plied their engines with a skill, extraordinary.

The scene was at once sublime and terrific. The light was sufficiently vivid to render the Jersey shore perfectly distinguishable; the agitated water reflected the flames like a mirror, the island—the shipping—two or three sloops sailing by; the steamboats, and the houses, roofs and steeples of all standing out in bold relief presented a picture of a truly remarkable and exciting character.

We shall, on Monday, be able to give more important particulars of the fire, and **conjectures as to its origin.**

---

from slumber, after, perhaps, a day of wearying toil and harassing vexations—to confront the direst extremes of cold and heat—to brave the 'pitiless pelting' of the storm—to face the raging element, that is their remorseless and tremendous antagonist—to dare almost every imaginable peril without the prospect of reward, or of promotion, or even of renown and glory—they should certainly make heroes, when fame and victory beckon them onward."

The excitement of chasing the engines was well told by Basil Hall, a visiting British sea captain, in 1829: "I succeeded by quick running in getting abreast of a fire engine; but although it was a very ponderous affair, it was dragged along smartly by its crew of some six-and-twenty men, aided by a whole legion of boys, all bawling as loud as they could, so that I found it difficult to keep up with them. On reaching the focus of attraction, the crowd of curious persons like myself began to thicken, while the engines came dashing in amongst us from every avenue, in the most gallant and business-like style. . . . The chief thing to find fault with on this occasion, were the needless shouts and other uproarious noises, which obviously helped to exhaust the men at the engines, and the needless forwardness, or it may be called fool-hardiness, with which they entered houses on fire, or climbed upon them by means of ladders, when it must have been apparent to the least skilful person, that their exertions were utterly hopeless. A small amount of discipline, of which, by the way, there was not a particle, might have corrected the noise."

That nobody slept through a fire is apparent from Captain Hall's report of another occasion: "I was scarcely well asleep again, before a second and far more furious alarm, brought all the world to the windows. The church bells were clanging violently at all hands, and the ear could readily catch, every now and then, a fresh sound chiming in with the uproar with much musical discord, and all speaking in tones of such vehemence as satisfied me that there would be no disappointment."

1839 Tabloid This is one of the earliest fire prints to appear in a newspaper on the very day of the blaze. The fire occurred in Philadelphia at 9 o'clock in the morning, and by 1 o'clock, an extra of the *Spirit of the Times* was in the streets with this wood-cut presentation. As the editor declared with becoming immodesty, "So much for enterprise!" The editor promised that "We shall, on Monday, be able to give more important particulars of the fire, and *conjectures as to its origins.*" *Historical Society of Pennsylvania*

Where a community had no fire alarm bell, a church bell was tolled. Even where there was a regular fire bell system, sextons usually were supposed to chime in with their church bells. Thus every volunteer fireman was sure to hear *some* bell. As for the townspeople, they couldn't sleep through a fire anyway, so they might just as well gravitate to the scene of the excitement. Even if they didn't like fires, they would meet all their friends.

Charles Dickens was a distinguished visitor to the United States. Subsequently he became the editor of a magazine called *All the Year 'Round*, which printed an article entitled "American Vol-

unteer Firemen" in its issue of March 16, 1861. Many scholars believe that this article was plainly from the pen of Dickens himself:

"But, after all, it is at night-time that the fireman is really himself, and means something. He lays down the worn-out pen, and shuts up the red-lined ledger. He hurries home from Lime-street, slips on his red shirt and black dress trousers, dons his solid japanned leather helmet bound with brass, and hurries to the guard-room, or the station, if he be on duty.

"A gleam of red, just a blush in the sky, east-ward—William-street way—among the warehouses; and presently the telegraph begins to work. For,

A Baltimore Warehouse Fire This painting by an unknown artist shows the burning of the warehouse of Henry Webb and Company on March 18, 1827. The respectable distance maintained by the firemen from the doomed structure shows that a wall collapse was anticipated. The engine in the center foreground has developed quite a powerful stream. *Maryland Historical Society*

Foreman's Trumpet This handsomely chased speaking trumpet was used by the foreman of Columbia Hose Company #1 of Paterson, New Jersey. *Paterson Evening News*

every station has its telegraph, and every street has its line of wires, like metallic washing-lines. Jig-jag, tat-tat, goes the indicator: 'Fire in William-street, No. 3, Messrs. Harcastle and Co.'

"Presently the enormous bell, slung for the purpose in a wooden shed in the City Park just at the end of Broadway, begins to swing and roll backward.

"In dash the volunteers in their red shirts and helmets—from oyster cellars and half-finished clam soup, from newly begun games of billiards, from the theatre, from Boucicault, from Booth, from the mad drollery of the Christy minstrels, from stiff quadrille parties, from gin-slings, from bar-rooms, from sulphurous pistol galleries, from studios, from dissecting rooms, from half-shuttered shops, from conversazioni and lectures—from everywhere—north, south, east, and west—breathless, hot, eager, daring, shouting, mad. Open fly the folding doors, out glides the new engine—the special pride of the company—the engine whose excellence many lives have been lost to maintain; 'A reg'lar high-bred little stepper' as ever smith's hammer forged. It shines like a new set of cutlery, and is as light as a 'spider waggon' or a trotting-gig. It is not the great Juggernaught car of our Sun and Phoenix offices—the enormous house on wheels, made as if purposely cumbrous and eternal—but is a mere light musical snuff-box of steel rods and brass supports, with axes and coils of leather, brass-socketed tubing fastened beneath, and all ready for instant and alert use.

"Now, the supernumeraries—the haulers and draggers, who lend a hand at the ropes—pour in from the neighboring dram-shops or low dancing rooms, where they remain waiting to earn some dimes by such casualties. A shout—a tiger!

"Hei! hei!! hei!!! hei!!!! (crescendo), and out at lightning speed dashes the engine, in the direction of the red gleam now widening and sending up the fanlike radiance of a volcano.

"Perhaps it is a steam fire-engine. They are entire successes, and will soon be universal among a people quick to grasp onward at all that is new, if it be but better than the old. Then the fires are lighted, and breathing out ardent smoke, and spitting out trails of fiery cinders; off it dashes.

"Now, a roar and crackle, as the quick-tongued flames leap out, red and eager, or lick the black blistered beams—now, hot belches of red-hot beams, as the floors fall in—now, burning stairs, like frightened martyrs running from the stake, rush poor women and children, in white trailing nightgowns—now, the mob, like a great exulting

The Night Alarm (*Above*) This N. Currier lithograph in "The Life of A Fireman" series shows a pumper about to leave its quarters to respond to a call. Immediately in front of the apparatus are John McDermott (who joined Currier's firm in the year of this picture, 1854) and John F. Sloper. *Museum of the City of New York*

Pick Up! (*Below*) There being little left in this building to burn, most of the firemen are preparing to return to their quarters in this Thomas & Wylie lithograph. But that was not the end of the night's work; there was dirty equipment to be cleaned. *Library of Congress*

many-headed monster, shouts with delight and sympathy—now, race up the fire-engines, the men defying each other in rivalry, as they plant the ladders and fire-escapes. The fire-trumpets roar out stentorian orders—the red shirts fall in line—rock, rock, go the steel bars that force up the water—up leap the men with the hooks and axes—crash, crash, lop, chop, go the axes at the partitions, where the fire smoulders. Now, spurt up in fluid arches the blue white jets of water, that hiss and splash, and blackens out the spasms of fire; and as every new engine dashes up, the thousands of up-turned faces turn to some new shades of reflected crimson, and half-broken beams give way at the thunder of their cheers."

Even the onlookers were carried away by the excitement of watching the firemen at work. In 1887, Augustine Costello recalled the scene as vying foremen shouted to their men: "The old-timer recollects well the music (enlivening to his ears) that followed these commands, and the young men of the present day can imagine how exciting it was to see twenty partially-stripped men (ten on a side) manning the brakes of a short-stroke engine and dashing her down at the rate of sixty or seventy strokes a minute, some with their hair floating about their faces at every stroke, while that of others was confined by closely-fitted skull-caps of red or striped flannel. Then upon the front of the engine the foreman would jump, and through his trumpet, or without the mouthpiece, shout to his men such stimulating cries as these: 'Every one of you, now, will you work?' 'Work her lively, lads!' 'You don't half work!' 'Now you've got her!' 'Stove her sides in!' 'Say you will, now!' and so on, his body swaying to the motion of the brakes, and

A Prison Fire New York's famous jail, "The Tombs," was the scene of this fire in 1842. The painting was made in the same year by H. B. Curtis. It was believed at the time that the fire had been set in order to effect the release of the brother of the renowned Samuel Colt, inventor of the revolver. As the inventor had been experimenting with explosives at that time, many people believed that the fire was a "plant."

Amidst the excitement, however, the prisoner committed suicide with a knife, aided, no doubt, by a book on anatomy that he had borrowed. In the foreground in this picture is Lady Washington Engine Company #40, known for obvious reasons as "The White Ghost." This company had many tough fighters, especially the semi-legendary Mose Humphrey, who feared neither fire nor fireman. *Insurance Company of North America*

Metamora Hose Company #29 This crack New York company, photographed in 1863, was made up primarily of merchants and their clerks. The 4-wheeled carriage was of rosewood, painted dark plum. The company name was that of the Indian hero of a play in which Edwin Forrest had starred. The restaurateur C. Delmonico belonged to this company. *H. V. Smith Museum of The Home Insurance Company*

he giving up only when his voice was gone, when some strong-bodied and loud-voiced member would relieve him. The men who worked on the brakes were tired now, and were in turn relieved in a minute or minute and a half, that being as long as a man could work on the brakes in that position, the labor being so violent and exhausting. But there were plenty on each side of the engine ready to fall in when the exhausted ones fell out, and as expert thing it was to fall in and catch the arm of the brake, between which and the box of the engine many a finger has been crushed, maiming a fire-laddie for life."

As one veteran recalled the day of the hand pumper, "The drumming of the engines in that line was music to the ear of the firemen, and tended to hurry him to the scene of the fight, or the fun, when blocks away."

NEW YORK'S FIRE OF 1835

New York has had innumerable fires, but the Great Fire of 1835 was the greatest (or the worst, depending upon how one looks at these things). It was the most serious municipal conflagration in an English-speaking community since the London fire of 1666.

The temperature was seventeen degrees below zero on the night of Wednesday, December 16. A private watchman discovered smoke coming from a five-story building, and he excitedly shouted his alarm. Out tumbled the firemen, still exhausted from their work at two serious fires in the past forty-eight hours. The burning structure was near the East River; but the water was frozen solidly, and the firemen had to chop holes in the ice for their hose lines. A gale drove streams from the nozzles back in the firemen's faces. But the smoke-eaters

New York's Great Fire of 1835 A group of prominent citizens asks Chief Engineer James Gulick about things. *National Board of Fire Underwriters*

had to keep pumping incessantly, for an engine would freeze if there were a moment's letup.

The flames could be seen a hundred miles away. Firemen came from Newark, New Jersey, by train. Four hundred firemen started from Philadelphia to help; as the railroad had not been completed all the way, part of the trip had to be made on foot. Men from the Benjamin Franklin and Northern Liberty hose companies arrived on Saturday morning, too late to help against the flames, although the Philadelphians did assist in "wetting down" the ruins. (In return, Putnam Hose Company No. 31 was to journey from New York to Philadelphia when the latter city had a bad fire in 1850.)

Meanwhile, the fire had been checked by desperate measures. Gunpowder was obtained from the United States Navy, and buildings in the path of the flames were blown up to create a firebreak.

The excitement and panic were compounded by thieves who set other fires in order to have better opportunity to plunder. One man was caught after he had started a fire, and citizens instantly lynched him.

James Gordon Bennett wrote this description for the New York *Herald* of December 18, 1835: "It was heartrending in the extreme. I walked down William Street. Crowds of people of both sexes were wandering in the same direction. It was piercing cold, and every other person had a woollen comforter wrapped around his neck. . . . United States soldiers were stationed here and there to protect the goods, yet the boys, men and women, of all colors, were stealing and pilfering as fast as they could. . . . The street was full of boxes and goods. I felt quite cold. I saw a large group of men stirring up a fire in the center of Wall Street, between Water and Front, which is here wide. On going near to warm myself I found the fire was made out of the richest merchandise and fine furniture from some of the elegant counting rooms. . . .

"From the corner of Wall Street I proceeded southwardly, for I cannot now talk of streets; all their sites are buried in ruins and smoking bricks. . . . I could not get further than a short distance down Front from the corner of Wall. The smoke, ruins, hot bricks, and all were to horrible to get over or through. . . . From the center of this street, looking to the left over the buildings in the direction of William, I saw nothing but flames ascending to heaven, and prodigious clouds of smoke curling after it as if from a volcano. . . . I beheld the several blocks of seven story houses, full of rich merchandise, on the northern side of the slip, in one bright, burning, horrible flame. About forty buildings were on fire at one moment. . . . On falling in with several of our most respectable citizens, I said, 'Awful! horrible!' 'Truly, truly,' said they, 'we are all ruined. . . . New York is put back twenty years. Philadelphia and Boston will now start ahead of us.' . . ." (Thirty-four years later, Reporter-Editor Bennett was to endow the James Gordon Bennett Medal for the New York Fire Department, after his Washington Heights home had been destroyed by a fire.)

Property damage was twenty million dollars, with 674 buildings being destroyed on seventeen blocks in a fifty-acre area in the center of the city. More than six hundred mercantile firms were dislodged. The fire was one of the precipitating causes of the suspension of payments by many banks. The fire also was one of the causes of the great Panic of 1837.

CURRIER & IVES

No one ever has caught the pulsating excitement of volunteer firemen at work so well as the artists of Currier & Ives. There was a logical reason for this. Nathaniel Currier, the founder of the firm, was himself a volunteer fireman. He belonged to Engine Company No. 2 in New York. And in many

The Great Fire of 1835 Flames finally have reached the Merchants' Exchange in Wall Street, one of New York's largest and finest structures. *National Board of Fire Underwriters*

GREAT FIRE AT ST LOUIS, M?
THURSDAY NIGHT MAY 17TH 1849.

23 Steam Boats and Cargoes destroyed, Valued at $468,000.

Total amount of property destroyed, estimated at $5,000,000

Value of Buildings destroyed $502,290.

St. Louis' Great 1849 Fire N. Currier made this lithograph of St. Louis' destructive water-front conflagration. *National Board of Fire Underwriters*

respects, the old-time volunteer firemen and Currier & Ives are inseparable.

When he was twenty-two, Currier formed his own lithography company. In that year occurred New York's Great Fire of 1835, and the young businessman promptly capitalized upon this melancholy event (a phrase that was to be used as part of the title of many of his scenes of catastrophe). Four days after the fire appeared the N. Currier lithograph entitled "Ruins of the Merchants' Exchange N.Y. After The Destructive Conflagration of Dec ᵇʳ 16 & 17, 1835." The speed with which this print reached the streets was phenomenal for that day.

In 1857, the firm's bookkeeper, Ives, became a partner, and the company's name was changed from N. Currier to Currier & Ives.

The six large folio prints of "The Life of a Fireman" series are probably the best-known American fire pictures that exist. The detail was fantastic; many of the faces depicted were actual portraits, and models were used to obtain exact features of the fire apparatus. These prints originally were sold for three dollars each. Somewhat less known is "The American Fireman" series; Fireman Currier himself posed for the print entitled "Always Ready." The price of these prints was $1.25 each. Far behind in popularity is the comic series, "The Darktown Fire Brigade."

The company also made fireman's membership certificates, with blank spaces for insertion of an individual smoke-eater's name, rank, and company. For the sentimental trade, there were pictures of seraph-faced children wearing helmets. Other lithographs were produced by the firm to show the great fires at Pittsburgh, Richmond, Chicago, Boston, and St. Louis.

ST. LOUIS' FIRE OF 1849

St. Louis, Missouri, was a thriving community in 1849, and the waterfront was crowded with shipping on May 17. That night, a fire (believed to have been the work of an incendiary) broke out on the ship *White Cloud*, which was tied to a wharf between Wash and Cherry streets. Before the flames could be subdued, they had spread to the vessels lying immediately to the port and starboard, the *Endors* and the *Edward Bates* (Missouri's Edward Bates was to decline the post of Secretary of War the following year, but eventually he became Lincoln's first Attorney General).

In an effort to save the wharves, sailors set the *Edward Bates* adrift; but the ship floated into the shore and set the levee afire. Flames ran up the hemp cables of other craft that were tied to piers and caused ship after ship to drift against wood-walled vessels. In a very short space of time, the entire waterfront was ablaze. Within thirty minutes, there was an unbroken line of fire for a mile.

Freight on the levee was ignited by wooden planking, and warehouses caught fire from the resultant flames. St. Louis was characterized by very narrow streets at that time, so that even without a breeze, the fire was easily able to jump across the roadways. Only when a wide clearing, such as Market Square, intervened could the blaze be held in check; hose streams could not contain the fire where other fuel could be seized upon by the flames.

By the following day, twenty-three steamships had been destroyed, as well as uncounted barges and small craft. The wharves were a shambles, and fifteen blocks of the city had been ravaged. The fire loss was estimated to be six million dollars.

But that was not the end of St. Louis' troubles. Overcrowding as a result of the fire losses made the community a fertile place for an epidemic of cholera, which came from Europe via New Orleans. The general collapse of municipal authority that resulted from the great fire prevented the assertion of any supervisory control until it was too late to isolate the afflicted persons.

A Worker in St. Louis (*Opposite*) The burning of the Pavilion on the Big Mound in 1848. The fire appears to be out of hand. Two hose companies and another engine company are bringing assistance. *Missouri Historical Society*

Fireman Currier The founder of Currier & Ives was a volunteer fireman, and he was the model of this 1858 lithograph entitled "Always Ready" in "The American Fireman" series. *H. V. Smith Museum of The Home Insurance Company*

FRIENDSHIP FIRE COMPANY
Nº 3.

Instituted
A.D. 1785.

Incorporated
A.D. 1839.

This Certifies that Frederick L. Fischer is a Member of the Friendship Fire Company, Nº 3, of Baltimore.

The Pride of Belonging

Inasmuch as a volunteer fire company was a civic responsibility, a social club, an energy outlet, and a place where much time had to be spent, a fireman regarded his group with far from unprejudiced eyes. His company was the best outfit in the whole community. His engine was the most beautiful, the most efficient, and the most *human* equipment in the land. His fellows were the noblest, swiftest, and toughest beings on earth. Let him who said to the contrary be prepared to prove it!

Some fire companies selected their men with great care, and it was a mark of distinction to belong to such a group. Around the mid-point of the nineteenth century, one girl wrote of her brother in her diary: "When he was twenty-one years old he joined a fire company, and it was called 'The Silk Stocking Hose Company' because so many young men of our best families were in it. But they didn't wear their silk stockings when they ran with the engine, for I remember seeing my brother one night when he came home from a fire and he had on a red flannel shirt and a black hat that looked like pictures of helmets the soldiers wear."

Yet the men of companies which were anything but aristocratic felt just as strongly about the advantages of belonging to their particular outfits. A volunteer who was born in 1799 said that "a fireman thought more of his engine than he did of his family." (He probably saw more of his en-

A Baltimore Fireman's Certificate
This certificate, complete with an illustration of the company's own apparatus, was issued by Friendship Fire Company #3. *Peale Museum, Baltimore*

gine, but familiarity did not breed contempt.) When an engine outpumped a rival company, the gloating firemen would fondly kiss their darling; and when a pumper was "washed" by another one, strong men would break down and cry like babies.

In 1894, a Detroit witness recorded that "the younger generation can have no proper appreciation of the social and political value attaching to a membership in a fire company in the days of the 'goose neck.'" A New York fireman who later became chief engineer recalled that "many and many a time have I worked my breath out while pumping old Thirteen, and lain in the street, and jumped up again and seized the brakes, because there was no one to take my place." This was a devotion that few men of that day acknowledged to their family or business.

A man had occasion to associate with the company of his choice not only at fires. There were regular monthly business meetings, there was participation in numerous parades, there were target matches. A fire company usually gave two or three balls and picnics a year. Holidays such as the Fourth of July or Christmas were customarily celebrated "with the boys." There was good reason why many wives were fiercely jealous of the fire companies. But there is no authenticated record of a spurned wife's having sought to disfigure this new object of her husband's affections, even though axes were readily available.

Many authenticated stories were told of the tough choice that a certain fireman would have to make: for example, wedding bells or fire bells? One New York fireman literally left his bride at the altar in order to heed the tocsin, and he did not return for three days. "What was a fellow going

Robt Tempest and Jos. Barton,
President & Vice President,
of the
HIBERNIA ENGINE Cº.

Engraved, Printed and Colored expressly for the Firemen's Magazine by Stott & Martin

Hibernia's Officers Here are the officers of the company shown in the following illustration. *Philadelphia Contributorship*

to do?" he asked simply; "let the engine get passed?" It is pleasant to relate that his bride ultimately forgave him.

Pride in one's company transcended even life itself, if the account of a witness is to be credited. A volunteer fireman visited a companion who was confined in New York's Old House of Refuge with consumption, incurred, no doubt, at a fire. "Oh, Jake!" exclaimed the caller, "could I but be in your place this moment, it would be happiness to what I now suffer." The sick man anxiously asked for details. "Jake, the engine got washed today." "Dick, who washed her?" "Twelve Engine." "Then let me die," replied Jake, "for I envy not your hold on life." And he expired at that very moment.

In 1886, one man recalled the great days of the volunteers, and he wrote that "it was no uncommon thing to see the old solid citizens in their broadcloth and gold-rimmed spectacles tugging at the ropes, really being dragged, while appearing to drag the painted and burnished absurdity to the fire."

More than one volunteer fireman failed in business because he spent too much time with his engine. Then the boys would try to get him a political or other appointment; and so great was the influence of the firemen in many communities that the bankrupt hero would get some political plum.

Some persons are natural "joiners" and a fire company was something to join if other opportunities were not present. In about 1817, it was related that a young man desired to join a certain church in New York, but he was told that he would have to wait out a two months' probationary period. Some time later, the pastor met this man and told him that he would now be accepted as a member. But the youth replied that he now had another affiliation: a fire company. "You see I was bound to join something, and these fellows let me in without any probation."

Some firemen refused the opportunity of becoming an officer, in a newly formed company, for they preferred to remain rank-and-file members of their old crew. The company title meant more than the individual's. Even if a man moved to a new neighborhood, he generally ran with his less convenient old company.

Hibernia Fire Engine Company #1

This Philadelphia company was organized in 1752, with a complement largely of Irishmen. Many patriots were members during the Revolutionary War. This print, made in 1757, shows the men in their green parade hats and capes. *Insurance Company of North America*

Even though Americans hated uniforms other than for military purposes (and many hated them too), exception was made in the case of firemen. The smoke-eaters did not wear the uniforms of a community fire department, for there was no such organization; each company was a separate entity. Therefore, a fireman proudly wore the uniform of his own particular company. In 1806, the costume of the Philadelphia Hose Company was described in these words: "consisting of a shirt of net-work, woolen drawers from the loins to the ancles, and a short frock coat of dark steel mixed cloth, with a painted cape and belt, suitably inscribed, these with the hats, constituted the first fireman's equipments."

The men of Protection Engine Company No. 5 of New York adopted the red flannel shirt as their

HIBERNIA FIRE ENGINE COMPANY. N°1.
OF PHILADELPHIA

Hibernia Fire Engine Co. No 1. of Philad'a to Washington Fire Co No 5. of
Charlestown, Mass, in remembrance of Auld Lang Syne.

PROTECTOR ENGINE Nº 2.

Fashion Plates These men of Protector Engine Company #2 of New York are wearing the red shirts that were to become the fireman's trademark. The shields were intended to be chest protectors as well as advertisement. Time: the early 1850's. Helmets were worn socially in that day. *National Board of Fire Underwriters*

uniform in 1840. The volunteer firemen were an individualistic, free-thinking lot, but here was something upon which they all could agree. Henceforth a fireman had to wear a red shirt. It was a badge. It was a fraternity pin. And the red shirt was said to attract the eyes of females as well as of bulls. In 1860, the *New York Times* explained that "young women consider the red shirts and black inexpressables the finest uniforms in the world."

The fireman's red shirt not only spread through the country; it even crossed the seas. In 1849, the great Italian patriot Garibaldi was living in exile in Staten Island, New York, where he earned his living as a ship's chandler while he plotted further revolutions. When he saw the red shirts of the firemen, he got the idea for the uniform of a quickly assembled militia. So when he was able to return to Italy and to organize his troops, he led

a band that has gone down into history as the Red Shirts.

American firemen also adopted the leather fire helmet as a uniform, even for parades and sometimes social use. The first leather helmet was made in New York in 1740. In about 1830, iron wire brims were sewn into the leather. By 1836, the fire helmet had acquired a close approximation of its present appearance: a long rear projection to protect the neck, a brass ornament (usually an eagle) to hold the name or number of the fireman's company. Dress helmets of precious materials became almost as popular as speaking trumpets for gifts to distinguished chief engineers or foremen.

Some fire companies had ornate leather belts as distinguishing gear. Other companies adopted suspenders (usually red) with the company name or number prominently displayed.

A Night Alarm This painting by E. Boehl shows St. Louis Fire Company #4, in 1853. The words "St. Louis" on the pumper were unusual in that day, for the firemen identified themselves with a company and not with the community. Boasts such as "Cataract," heroes such as "Andrew Jackson," or slogans such as "Rough and Ready" were far more common names on fire engines. *Missouri Historical Society*

At a fire, the men generally would fraternize with firemen of other companies, all strictly in the line of duty. But after the flames had been subdued, each company's members would return to their house as a proud unit. Sometimes the men would go out for refreshments as a body.

> And when the fire was mostly quenched
> And smoke obscured the stars,
> Some trump with open heart would treat
> To lager and cigars!

Most companies awarded their members with handsome membership certificates, usually with a fireman-save-my-child motif. The certificate might be the only tangible reward for a lifetime of service and hazard. Thus it was a treasure to be prized above any other possession. Today, when one occasionally finds a fireman's certificate in an attic it is not unusual to find that the fireman or his family had pasted his picture on the document.

Any reasonably able-bodied man could join some company. But to join a particular outfit was often a mark of great distinction. And the new man had to show that he was really a part of this company by service of an extracurricular nature, such as defending the honor of his comrades-in-arms. The emphasis was on the *arms*.

The Torchbearer (*Right*) Well-favored persons who were too young (or too old) to serve as firemen were honored with the post of torchbearer. With his ornate lamp, he led his company to the scene of the fire. *Smithsonian Institute*

A Baltimore Fire House (*Left*) Weccacoe Engine Company was very proud of its elegant quarters. *National Board of Fire Underwriters*

Get Out! (*Below*) In their zeal to get their engine out, several members of this company have not taken time to doff their dress clothes. Torchbearer at extreme left. Lithograph is by Thomas & Wylie. *Library of Congress*

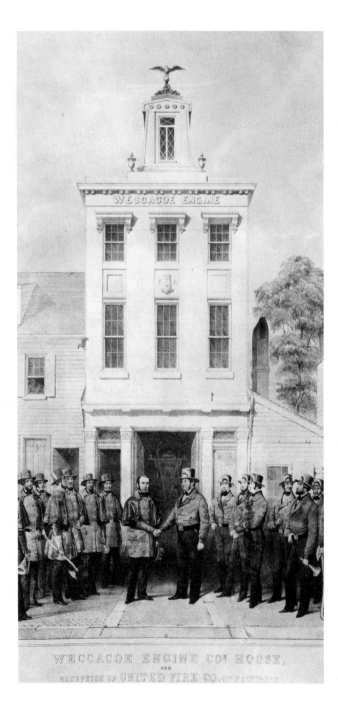

WECCACOE ENGINE CO. HOUSE,
AND
RECEPTION OF UNITED FIRE CO.

THE VOLUNTEER.

Volunteer Fireman, j. g. This 1857 Currier & Ives lithograph shows a fortunate youth who has achieved managerial status in his chosen profession.

Firemen
and Community Life

Help for Fire Victims Volunteers firemen took care not only of fires, but of the victims of fires. This scene shows what often happened in a fire house after the flames had been subdued. Dispossessed persons were given shelter and food. In case of need, the firemen would even supply funds (their own).

The volunteer firemen were definitely "of the people, by the people, for the people." They made themselves a prominent and vital part of community life, fire fighting as such being merely one facet of this activity. One writer noted in 1837 that "such vast interests and such important consequences depend upon the cheerful activity and cordial exertions of the firemen in discharge of their almost thankless duty."

Americans always have been characterized by generosity, and the volunteer firemen were outstanding among the generous. One old company had as its motto, *Haud ignara mali, miseris succurrere disco* (Not unacquainted with misfortune, I have learned to succor the needy)." It mattered little that most of the firemen never had heard of Virgil or of Dido and Aeneas. Before the days of organized charity, the needy were helped only by those who were personally familiar with the needy. And, in the case of persons who were rendered homeless or destitute by the flames, that meant the firemen.

Persons who lost their homes or clothing were taken by the smoke-eaters to their own firehouses, while efforts were made to supply what had been lost. The firemen took care not only of the widows and families of their fallen comrades; they often raised purses to take care of persons whose lives they just had saved. "Specials" given by the firemen frequently were for the benefit, not of themselves, but of persons who had sustained losses at fires. Tickets and announcements of such affairs sometimes were adorned with the picture of a fireman who was distributing money to the needy from the ample interior of his inverted leather helmet. That picture was more than symbolic.

It was not surprising that the smoke-eaters were so generous with mere money. They were overly generous with their time, limbs, and lives.

The hard-toiling, virile firemen were usually tough men on a bottle, but, interestingly enough, there were some "dry" groups among the smoke-eaters. In 1840, the Temperance Society in New York made efforts to interest the firemen, and several companies signed up as complete units. One member of Engine Company No. 18 thus rationalized his position: "Why shouldn't we join the temperance movement? Are we not of all men the most steadfast believers in the efficacy of water? Why, we could not get along without water. It is our native element, and may we always have enough of it."

In appraising the smoke-eaters, one writer declared in 1860: "To sum up all, the Fireman is a generous friend, a good citizen, and a disinterested philanthropist." A minister delivered a sermon entitled "Show Thyself a Man" to Brooklyn smoke-eaters in 1862, and he posed this tantalizing question: "Can a man be a Christian and a Fireman?" It is pleasing to record that his answer was yes.

A number of plays was written with smoke-eater heroes. Samuel D. Johnson's *The Fireman* was first performed in Boston in 1849, with many performances in other cities of the land. On the title page appears the theme of the play: "The noble Fireman is here represented in his true character—an honest, heroic, and charitable man, fearless of danger when duty calls, and whose motto is, 'IMPELLED BY EMULATION AND ACTUATED BY BENEVOLENCE.'"

NO 1.

THE EMPIRE HOOK & LADDER POLKA

COMPOSED BY

Prof. HENRY C. THUNDER

Dedicated with esteem

TO

W^m. F. SMITH ESQ. PRESIDENT.

BY HIS FRIEND

OZEAS H. RAMBORGER.

Philadelphia, A. FIOT, N° 196, Chesnut S^t   New York, Hall & Son, Broadway.

Dedicated with Esteem The composer of this polka in 1852 dedicated it to his favorite firemen, the crew of Empire Hook & Ladder Company #1 of Philadelphia. Note the speaking trumpets and lanterns. *National Board of Fire Underwriters*

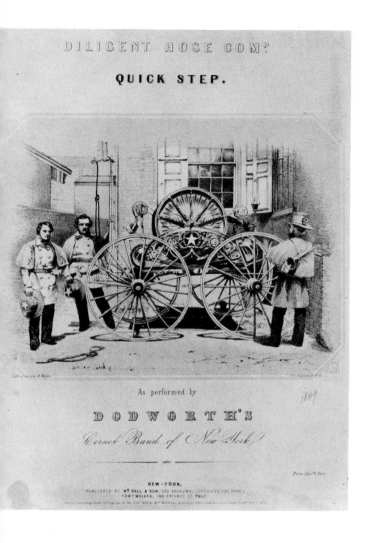

1849 Sheet-Music A hose company was a particularly suitable illustration for a quick-step. The imaginative publisher may not have had any particular company in mind, however, for the music was issued in New York, but the Diligent Hose Company was not a New York fire company. The uniform (which was not in the New York manner) is more suggestive of Philadelphia or Baltimore. *National Board of Fire Underwriters*

Little Hero When Currier & Ives made this lithograph in 1859, junior space-men had not been invented. There was still enough glamour here on earth. *National Board of Fire Underwriters*

Composers devoted not a little of their talent to writing songs to the volunteer firemen. "The Fireman's Bride" contained these words:

> *Who wouldn't be a fireman's darling?*
> *Who wouldn't like to be a fireman's bride?*
> *I'm going to be a fireman's lover.*
> *I'm going to be a fireman's wife.*

Less delicate was "The Quadrille Fire-Set," which was orchestrated for various instruments, including a fire bell.

Some songs were more particularized, as this one which appeared in the book *The Providence Fireman* in 1886:

> *Peal out ye Fire bells in a dreaded tone,*
> *The Firemen will protect the property we own.*
> *Let the fiery flames leap high in the air,*
> *The Providence Firemen will do and dare.*

A Song for the Hooksies As community heroes, firemen were logical enough dedicatees for song writers. A Baltimore company was honored with this number. *National Board of Fire Underwriters*

Other songs had a particular company as their objective:

. . . No fatal fang shall wound you,
The Fireman's wary eye
Shall be a guard around you
Oceana's men are nigh.

In the heyday of the minstrels, topical verses were very popular. The burning of a hotel in one city produced a lament that was concluded with these words:

Oh, Heaven, what a pity, in this great and
noble City,
That such accidents should happen to decry
its honest fame.
And when evidence is sifted, authorities'
hands uplifted,
They bring in a verdict, "There's no one to
blame."

After the loss of one building, a minstrel sang:

To subdue the angry demon, every steamer
had a stream on;
To save the massive structure all efforts were
in vain.

The firemen themselves sometimes turned their fingers to the lyre. Their efforts usually were aimed at self-aggrandizement. One crew of smoke-eaters liked to sing these words upon their return from a fire (en route to the blaze, of course, one's breath had to be conserved):

We are coming back rejoicing,
The liveliest boys you've seen;
We beat them other fellers
At the fire we painted green.

Other songs were devised for the particular benefit of some rival company:

The silver hook and ladder,
The pretty, golden Four,
To make Thirty-one the madder,
Wash the paint from off her door.

Another derisive verse declared:

There is an engine house,
Not far away,
Where they are last at fires,
Three times a day.

Every self-respecting fire company had a secretary, of course; but when one company actually selected an assistant secretary, that was too much for the bard of a rival crew, who wrote:

Number Six has come on deck
With a new assistant sec.,
Do ye mind?
He's as dirty as its water,
Tho' he thinks himself a snorter,
But he really hadn't oughter,
Do ye mind?

Just as sailors worked the capstan to music, so a few companies had music while they pumped at fires. Forest Engine Company No. 3 of New York had a genuine singer of Irish ballads for use at the scene of a conflagration.

Until athletics became of national interest at about the mid-point of the nineteenth century, the firemen participated in the substitutes for physical contests then known. There were marching drills, target shooting, and other activities in which the men could participate as an organized company: a fire company, that is. One of the world's earliest baseball clubs was organized in the house of Mutual Hook & Ladder Company No. 1 of New York on June 24, 1857; and because of its origin, this organization took the name of the Mutual Baseball Club. It participated in some of the first interclub contests ever held.

In the heyday of the volunteers, the term "visiting fireman" meant what it said, and firemen loved to travel as a company to call upon their fellow craftsmen in other communities. Sometimes the fire companies traveled to tournaments or to give an exhibition, but many of the visits were purely social. It was not at all unusual for firemen to go to Washington, with their apparatus, for presidential inaugurations; and they would wholeheartedly participate in the inaugural parades. Local rivalries were not present during these excursions, and firemen hosts and guests outdid themselves

in verbal gallantry at the banquet table. On one trip to Baltimore, a member of New York's Columbian Engine Company No. 14 declared that he had been looking for the Mason and Dixon line, but that he could not find it nor any other line that could separate the friendships of volunteer firemen. Baltimore's boys then frantically hunted for a speaker who could reply in kind to such oratory.

The participation of firemen in politics began early. Because of company loyalty, the firemen could usually be counted upon to vote as a bloc; and many a politician got his start as an organizer of firemen votes. The outstanding example was "Boss" Tweed, whose leadership of Tammany Hall was perhaps the high-water mark of political filth. His wiles were less successful when he was a volunteer fireman.

When Tweed was foreman of Americus Engine Company No. 6 in New York, his men participated in a spirited contest to see whether any pumper could project a stream of water above a tall new Liberty pole in front of Riley's saloon, at Franklin

Practical Politics James Gulick was one of the most colorful of New York's chief engineers. But when Tammany Hall refused to put him on the Democratic ticket as candidate for Register, the Whigs sponsored him. He won by the largest majority ever received by a local office seeker up to that time, even though the

Whigs were a minority party. One of the most effective campaign placards in this campaign read:

"Who saved the Cathedral?
JAMES GULICK
Vote for him for Register."

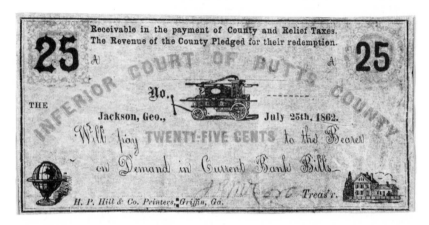

Prior to the enactment of the National Bank Act in February, 1863, any bank, financial institution, or other agency could print its own paper money, with only minimum restrictions by some of the states. Designs on these notes were varied: some showed the portraits of great men, while other bills depicted some object of general interest. The notes shown on this page all illustrate early types of fire engines.

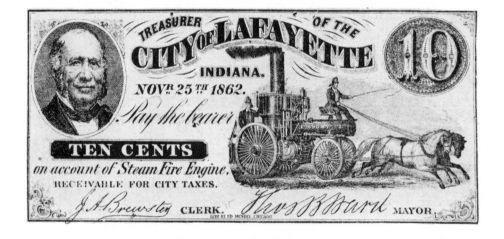

Street and West Broadway. Tweed's boys may have been politically inspired, but they were just about as good a company of firemen as the city then had. Their stream reached higher than those of competitors, but it was still three feet from the top of the pole. Amidst heavy wagers, Tweed promised to have his men shoot a stream over the pole on the following day. That night, the boss hired a sailor to climb Riley's pole and to saw off the top six feet; this was the day of the clipper ship, when seamen were familiar with lofty riggings. Tweed promised to pay ten dollars for the job, five dollars being paid on the spot. That night, the sailor surreptitiously climbed the pole. And on the next day, Americus Six again was able to wet the pole three feet from the top. The consistency was remarkable but Tweed's men lost their bets. In a towering rage, he sought out the sailor, who calmly explained that inasmuch as only half of the fee had been paid, only half of the pole had been severed.

Fireman Tweed left a permanent mark upon the American political scene. When he was foreman of Americus Six, that engine had painted on its box the head of a snarling Bengal tiger. Tweed carried this symbol with him to Tammany Hall, and the tiger is still the symbol of that political organization.

Firemen frequently served as an adjunct to the local police departments. The smoke-eaters helped the bluecoats to handle crowds at parades, funerals, and even riots.

It is not surprising that firemen have survived in the arts. The contributions of dramatists and composers have been mentioned. The heroic forms of firemen became prominent on weather vanes and clipper prows. The familiar helmeted profile adorned bandboxes and other personal effects. Paper money sometimes was adorned with engravings of fire engines. It all reflected on the importance of the fireman in community life. They were needed for fires—or other emergencies. But the indispensable smoke-eaters could not be kept from popping up in all sorts of places.

Tammany's Insignia This copy of a French lithograph was painted on the box of "Boss" Tweed's Americus Engine Company #6. *H. V. Smith Museum of The Home Insurance Company*

Translation of Psyche John Archibald Woodside painted this mythological scene as a panel for Americus Engine Company #6 of New York. _Insurance Company of North America_

Fire Engines as Works of Art

Originally, fire engines were utilitarian in nature and in appearance. But as men became fiercely loyal to their particular companies, the engines—the center of all activities—became the objects of much attention, affection, and adulation. It was but a logical next step for the men to dress up the equipment in the best possible finery.

One nineteenth-century scribe thus wrote of a fireman's attitude toward his engine: "He spoke of it in the feminine gender. He liked to see *her* look well, and hence his readiness to spend his money on the decoration of his engine."

At first the decoration of fire engines was on a strictly amateur basis, as was everything else connected with the fire departments. In time, however, the best artists in America did not consider it beneath their dignity to decorate the panels of the fire engines. Thomas Sully, Henry Inman, John A.

Woodside, John Vanderlyn, and David and Joseph Johnson were commissioned to do honor to the firemen. In a day when even railroad locomotives were individually decorated, the well-beloved fire engines were a magnificent outlet for an imaginative painter.

Many of the engines (particularly in the larger communities, where competition extended even into aesthetics) were wondrous to behold. Thus Niagara Engine Company No. 4 in New York had a white box ornamented with gold with a delicate shadow; the wheels were blue, well gilded; the pumping levers also were blue, "neatly ornamented." There were four paintings of Niagara Falls on the condenser case. On the gallery of 'the condenser were mottoes: "Duty Our Pleasure" and "Ever Ready, Ever Willing."

Niagara Engine Company #4 This well-decorated pumper was one of the show pieces of the New York volunteer firemen. Time: 1856.

The Pride of Charlestown Warren Engine Company #4 of Charlestown, Massachusetts, owned this apparatus. The engine, which was in use in 1861, was a very handsome piece of equipment with shining metal work and delicate ornamentation. *National Board of Fire Underwriters*

A Carriage Maker's Masterpiece Woodruff Hose Company #1 was the owner of this elegant hose reel. To facilitate the unwinding of the hose, a chain drive mechanism was used. Hose reels of this type were marvels of lightness. *American-LaFrance-Foamite Corporation*

Not to be outdone, the rival Live Oak Engine Company No. 44 had a box carved out of solid mahogany for the condenser, with corners surmounted by Turks' heads, topped by live oak trees with the branches running over and intertwining with each other, while wooden squirrels perched on branches. On the panels were two pilot boats, carved out of solid wood. The box of the engine was painted blue, a shade lighter than ultramarine.

Franklin Company of Philadelphia had its engine decorated with scenes from the life of Benjamin Franklin: arriving in the city as a youth with a loaf of bread under his arm, serving as a fireman, sitting at his desk, and the like.

Even the less ornate hose companies found possible means of adornment. New York's Hose Company No. 5 had its running gear painted a lake color striped with gold, while the hose reel was elegantly carved, the ironwork being entirely silver-plated, with the municipal coat of arms in solid silver on side shields. Hose Company No. 9 was the first to introduce bells on the carriage, although this was considered foppish at the time.

Amity Hose Company No. 38 boasted of the most expensive hose carriage in the land: hard wood it was, painted snow-white, very heavily mounted with silver, with red glass lamps (shaped like pineapples) mounted in gold on the sides.

One company spent five hundred dollars for a single lamp. Another outfit spent a thousand dollars for a picture for the back of its engine. A hose company that was named after a race horse ("Fashion") was decorated accordingly: the lifters of the hose reel represented horses' heads, the jaws of which opened when the lids were raised.

The use of silver plate, gold leaf, and burnished brass was prodigal.

Paintings on equipment showed scenes of patriotism, heroism, mythology, or unadorned beauty. One company selected a portrait of an actor; another company, the Three Graces; yet another, a pirate. One morbid crew had a painting of the firemen's cemetery at Greenpoint, New York. Some companies had historical documents painted on their apparatus. Certain engines were adorned with realistic battle scenes.

The Emblem of Tammany Hall This engine was acquired by Americus Engine Company #6 of New York in 1851. Its most celebrated foreman was William Marcy ("Boss") Tweed; and when he became the head of Tammany Hall, the Democrats took as their symbol the tiger's head that may be seen painted upon the front panel of the engine. *Museum of the City of New York*

Squirrel Tail Pumper This engine was sometimes referred to as the "squirrel tail" type. The large suction tube was dropped into a cistern or river to draw water; this tube was permanently attached to the rear of the pumper, and it was maneuvered into place atop the engine when not in use. The pump handles likewise were carried high on the apparatus, but they could be swung down to a chest-high pumping position. *American-LaFrance-Foamite Corporation*

The Vigilant (*Above opposite*) This was one of the better known engines in Philadelphia in 1853. It was known as a Philadelphia style engine: that is, a folding platform to be seen over each wheel permitted a second tier of men to man the brakes. The engine was thus known as a double decker. A silver speaking (or yelling) trumpet betokens the foreman, later known as the captain. *National Board of Fire Underwriters*

A Study in Lightness This fragile-appearing hose reel could withstand a good deal of punishment, but it was light enough for rapid transportation. This vehicle is now in the Smithsonian Institute. *Smithsonian Institute*

Franklin (*Below opposite*) This painting of Franklin's famed experiment with a kite was made to serve as a panel for Franklin Engine Company of Philadelphia in about 1830. The artist is not known. *Insurance Company of North America*

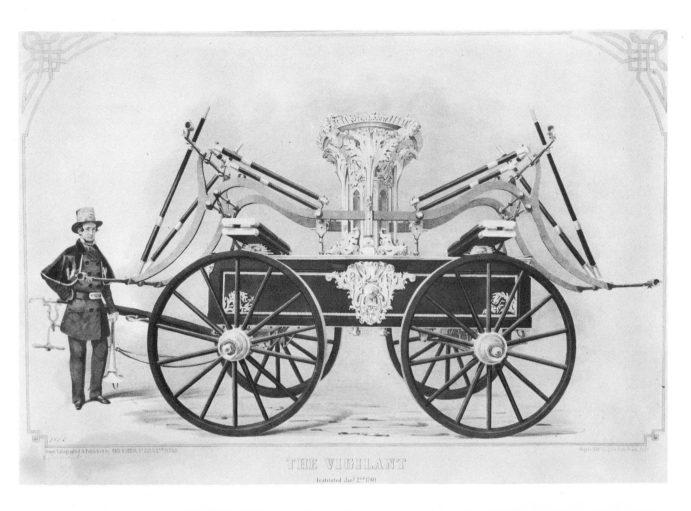

THE VIGILANT

Instituted Jan.? 2.nd 1760

HUMANE HOSE COMPANY,
N.º 4.
Instituted April 5th 1805
PHILAD.ª

Philadelphia Hose Reel This was the magnificent equipment of Humane Hose Company #4 of Philadelphia. Note the beautiful paint-work. *National Board of Fire Underwriters*

HIBERNIA ENGINE,
COMP. N°1,
instituted 1732

The lavishness of engine adornment is even more to be wondered at when one realizes that the firemen paid for this work out of their own pockets. A volunteer fireman risked not only his life; he risked his purse. Occasionally the friends of a particular company would add to the collection or assessment. Or the panels might be donated by a relatively wealthy admirer. Sometimes a company that helped out the sorely pressed smoke-eaters of another community would be "thanked" with paintings to be attached to the engine.

Most susceptible of adornment was the gooseneck pumper, which had a high box that could serve as the resting place of paintings. It was rumored that some companies voted not to change their apparatus to the more powerful "hay wagon" type because the latter was too functional to permit much artwork.

The *Fireman's Herald* thus apostrophized an engine on March 9, 1882:

> Behold! How she shines in her beauty,
>   Resplendent in silver and gold;
> Ne'er shrinking from doing her duty,
>   When worked by her members so bold;
> So peacefully-innocent standing,
>   You'd dream not the work she can do,
> But when we her aid are demanding,
>   She always proves faithful and true.

Hibernia Engine Company #1 This distinguished Philadelphia company (formed in 1752) owned this handsome engine. The brightly-painted scenes on the panels were well set off by the bright paint and polished metal trimmings of the rig. *Philadelphia Contributorship*

Lafayette The distinguished artist Thomas Sully painted this panel for the Lafayette Hose Company of Philadelphia in 1833. *Insurance Co. of North America*

BURNING OF THE NEW YORK CRYSTAL PALACE,
on Tuesday Oct. 5th 1858.
DURING ITS OCCUPATION FOR THE ANNUAL FAIR OF THE AMERICAN INSTITUTE.

The Crystal Palace Fire This Currier & Ives lithograph shows the burning of the Crystal Palace in New York in 1858. The fire was to wreck this handsome edifice. *National Board of Fire Underwriters*

The American Institute Fair gave prizes for the most handsome fire engines, and the competition was tremendous. The Fair of the American Institute at Castle Garden, New York, gave diplomas to the best examples of the art. At many exhibitions and fairs, there was competition in beauty as well as performance of the engines.

In part, the manufacturers of fire engines were responsible for the ornate character of the apparatus. Beauty was a fine selling point in itself. Moreover, a volunteer fire company which had an engine that was highly serviceable but highly undecorative might be persuaded that a new piece would help the company's prestige. Sometimes, upon its anniversary, a company would purchase a fine new "show piece." Yet even beauty was not enough to dim the memory of the old apparatus to some men. When Pacific Engine Company No. 14 in New York acquired a bright new replacement, a fireman sadly wrote:

While the new lady is our boast,

The old one in our hearts shall live.

Some companies had removable panels on their engines, so that works of art could be spared the rigors of day-to-day service. Other outfits had special fancy equipment for parades, but ordinary "crabs" were used for extinguishing fires. Yet if an alarm sounded during a parade, the most elaborate apparatus was recklessly exposed to flames, smoke, water, and the assaults of jealous rivals.

Many volunteers made a habit of carrying chamois in their pockets. Then, whenever a speck of dust appeared on their engine, a quick polishing job could be performed instanter. One company employed a giant Negro to march alongside its machine on parades, to flick his duster for any descending dirt.

That there was an obvious conflict between the utilitarian nature of the fire engine and the artistic character of the adornment bothered no one. There was no unity of style. But suppose an ugly gooseneck nozzle protruded from a lovely gold and purple painting; was not the volunteer fireman of that day also a split personality of utterly different facets?

THE CRYSTAL PALACE FIRE

So elegant were certain of the hand-drawn fire engines that they were exhibited as works of art. Some of the machines were centers of attraction even at such a museum as the Crystal Palace.

New York's magnificent Crystal Palace was opened on July 14, 1853, for the exhibition of the industry of all nations. Today it would be known as a World's Fair. The palace was located next to the aqueduct at Fifth Avenue and Forty-second Street, on land that once had been the municipal potter's field.

"The fairy-like Greek cross of glass, bound together with withes of iron, with its graceful dome, its arched naves, and its broad aisles and galleries, filled with choice productions of art and manufactures, gathered from the most distant parts of the earth, quaint old armor from the Tower of London, gossamer fabrics from the looms of Cashmere, Sèvres china, Gobelin tapestry, Indian curiosities, stuffs, jewelry, musical instruments, carriages, and machinery of home and foreign manufacture, Marochetti's colossal statue of Washington, Kiss's Amazon, Thorwaldsen's Christ and the Apostles, Powers's Greek Slave, and a host of other works of art beside, will long be remembered as the most tasteful ornament that ever graced the metropolis." The structure contained 1,250 tons of iron and 39,000 square feet of glass.

At five o'clock on the afternoon of October 5, 1859, smoke was seen near one entrance. Some two thousand persons fled by means of an exit a block away. The timing of the fire (the work of an incendiary) was fortunate; ten thousand persons would have been in the structure that night.

The volunteer firemen responded in force, but twenty or thirty streams of water had little effect on the roaring inferno. In half an hour, the structure was a molten mass of ruins. Some precious jewels were saved. And the firemen made particularly valiant efforts to save some of the handsome fire apparatus that was on display in the palace, two ornate hose carriages being salvaged. Several primitive steamers, which could not be used to fight for their own lives, were lost.

The damage toll was two million dollars. It was New York's worst conflagration since 1853, when a general alarm fire had destroyed the plant and warehouses of the publishing firm of Harper & Brothers. At that fire, Engine Company No. 7 was commanded, as usual, by Foreman Fletcher Harper, a partner in the publishing firm.

The Harper & Brothers Fire This view of the great publishing house fire appeared in the *London Illustrated News.*

The Sheer Joy of

In a day almost lacking in athletic competition and social contests, the incidents of fire fighting made up the void for many men. At first the volunteer firemen wanted merely to extinguish the fire; then they wanted to do so before rival companies could. When a man devoted the major portion of his time and effort to his company, he wanted to be sure that other companies were regarded in an inferior light.

Rivalries were not a characteristic merely of the fire departments in the larger communities. If there were two or more companies, there automatically was somebody else to beat. Thus fierce competition

began in Pittsburgh in 1811 with the organization of a *second* company, the Vigilants. A news item in a Reading, Pennsylvania, newspaper, in 1847 reported that "a misunderstanding between a few of the members of the Junior Engine and Hope Hose Companies ended in a battered nose on the one part, and a black eye on the other."

Oddly enough, it was the fire insurance companies and the most respectable citizens in town who innocently caused much of the rivalry. Such parties frequently offered cash prizes for the first company to reach the scene of the conflagration, or the first crew that actually got water on the flames. As early

The White Turtles and the Red Crabs Two traditional Philadelphia rivals race towards a fire in the 1840's. They never got there. The Northern Liberty Company (White Turtles) met the Lafayette Hose Company (Red Crabs) at Dillwyn and Noble Streets; and in a ferocious battle, the Turtles routed the Crabs. *Insurance Company of North America*

Fighting Each Other

as 1740, Boston offered a premium of five pounds to the company whose engine "shall first be brought to work" at each fire. A resolution of the Mutual Fire Insurance Company of Germantown, Pennsylvania, provided "that $3 be paid to the Engine Company that shall be first in operation in any Fire in which the Company is interested, and that the Secretary be instructed to furnish a copy to each of the Engine Companies in the Township of Germantown." This meant that "heroic" means were used to keep one's adversaries from getting there first. It might mean street fighting. It might mean racing one's engines on the more smoothly surfaced sidewalks, at great risk to pedestrians. It might mean sounding false alarms, to weary one's rivals so that they could not run so swiftly to a genuine fire.

At night, some volunteers dashed to fires in their night clothes, dressing after the engine was pumping water. The bunking system was devised at firehouses to get the apparatus to the scene of need before rival companies could do so. The tow ropes of engines were manned by any person who could be found, even elderly men or young boys. Engine Company No. 6 in New York actually had a runner who was a cripple. "He asked no odds of any one,

A Race The small "New York style" engine on the left should win this encounter, but perhaps a sudden "incident" will bring the race to a halt.

and when inside the ropes of the engine, his crutch seemed to be a living part of himself."

Seventy years ago, it was noted that "the present generation can hardly imagine the spirit and endurance exhibited in a race between fire companies in those days. Talk about horse racing and rowing matches—they vanish like bubbles into thin air, in comparison with the race of the firemen, each endeavoring to outdo his fellows in the strife to be first at the fire, first at work, and have first stream on."

If one company overtook another en route to a fire, the latter crew was said to be "passed," and this was a fearful disgrace. Sometimes a company, to avoid being overtaken, would weave erratically on the street, so that there was no room to get by. Often a collision would be engineered, or brawlers would attack the men of a fast-approaching company. In order to avoid the shame of having his company "passed," a foreman might shout to his

The Beginning of a Race This water color, made by S. W. Hill in 1830, shows City Hall and Park Row in New York. In the right foreground is Engine Company #44, better known as "Live Oak" by reason of the fact that most of its members were ship-builders. To be initiated, it is obvious that a spirited race is about to begin with the boys of Protection Engine Company #5 ("Old Honey Bee"), which may be seen on the left. The body of a pedestrian who did not get out of Honey Bee's way in time may be noted on the pavement behind the engine. *I. N. Phelps Stokes Collection*

men, "Stop and fix that wheel!" Technically his men were not passed (they had stopped for repairs!), but nobody was fooled.

On occasion, several companies would conspire to frame a victim, which was apt to be an outfit that was getting to be too efficient. A sham alarm was given, and the victim's apparatus would be hauled along the streets at breakneck speed. At various points along the way, fresh companies that had been lying in wait for this opportunity now ranged alongside of the wearied men of the victim and, in most instances, they would pass the panting laddies. Perhaps four fresh companies would pass an exhausted company in this manner; but on the record, the company unquestionably had been passed four times.

In order to prevent a rival from getting water on a fire before one's own company, men unencumbered with apparatus might dash to the scene with a barrel, which they would put over the nearest hydrant. While the men of the first company to arrive frantically looked for the hydrant, an innocent-looking person would sit on this barrel, which he would whip off when his own boys reached the scene. In Pittsburgh, "plug guards" were formed by some companies to reach and to hold the sources of supply until the regular firemen arrived with the engine.

At fires that were distant from the water supply, a common enough situation in the old days, it was usually necessary for several engines to pump in tandem: that is, an engine at the hydrant or cistern would pump into a second engine nearer the blaze, and the second machine would pump into a third, until ultimately the water could be pumped directly onto the flames. This was a great cause of rivalry. If a company could absorb more water in its pumper than another outfit could pump into it, the latter company was said to be "sucked." Even more of a disgrace was being "washed," which took place when a company could pump more water into the next engine in line than that apparatus could pump out again, with the result that the excess water overflowed from the "washed" engine. A company that never had been "washed" by another was proudly called an "old maid." Among the dozens of engines in New York in the volunteer days, only Engine Company No. 15 could boast of never having been "washed" by any company; and No. 15 was widely known as "Old Maid."

When Engine Company No. 13 in New York obtained a new pumper in 1835, the firemen promised that the foreman of the first company to "wash" them would get a new suit of clothes. Engine Company No. 11 won its foreman this finery

in a furious contest, during which the victor's men pumped from 130 to 150 strokes a minute; the pace was so terrific that no man could stay at the pump handles for more than fifteen seconds at a time.

Some forms of competition were innocent enough. Firemen loved to pump competitively at county fairs, militia musters, Fourth of July picnics, or any other occasion. At a time when other forms of competition were regarded as unproductively wasteful and thus immoral, the utilitarian nature of fire drills saved this form of rivalry from public disapproval. If there was no formal tournament, two companies might meet beside a tall pole or church spire to compare streams of water. In Reading, Pennsylvania, for example, a favorite

measuring rod was the spire of the Trinity Lutheran Church, 125 feet high; for horizontal tests, Penn Square was used.

But in time the rivalries became more savage, vicious. Ruffians disengaged the hose lines of other companies at fires or severed the lines; bullies damaged competitors' equipment or made personal assaults upon other firemen. In vain did municipal authorities fine or suspend the offenders, for others would "avenge" them. Men frequently were recruited solely for their skill as street fighters. Engine Company No. 15 in New York had a one-armed man, who kept a paving stone in his armless sleeve; certainly he had not been selected for his ability to pull a heavy engine.

The typical fireman of the old volunteer era was generally a doughty street fighter. Certainly the most imitated, if not the most admired, was the semilegendary Moses Humphreys. He was a loafer, a brawler, and a bully; but he also was a fireman without equal. He was said to be eight feet tall, give or take a couple of inches, and the high beaver hat which usually surmounted his flaming red hair made him look even taller. His hands were characterized as hams. His feet were cased in spiked shoes, for fighting (body-jumping) purposes. Humphreys generally headed the tow rope of Lady Washington Engine Company No. 40 in New York, and no one got in his way. If he could not find a hydrant available upon arriving at a fire,

A Pumping Contest This is a fire engine contest at Market and Fifth Streets in Philadelphia in 1850. The firemen were fiercely competitive, and they proudly wore their parading regalia even in contests. *Insurance Company of North America*

64

A Boston Contest This scene shows a friendly match between smoke-eaters on the Boston Common in 1851. But the "friendly" contest might end up in a brawl.

he would yank out the hose of an earlier arrival. And if anyone dared to challenge this giant, there was no containing of his wrath. He would snatch the shaft from a passing wagon and furiously belabor his foes with this weapon. Or he would tear a paving stone from a roadway and get to work. But brawler or not, he was a real fireman. One eyewitness recorded that "he would plunge into a burning house and bring out in his arms helpless women and children, and stand on top of a ladder, with the flames all around him, enacting exploits of the most prodigious peril and valor; and the people loved him and went to see him, thronging the theatre wherever he appeared."

In 1849, this fearsome smoke-eater became the prototype of a character in a play called *A Glance*

At New York. The play was a tremendous hit. But not everyone approved of the swaggering hero, and one critic complained that "the effect of this character upon juveniles who visit the theatre is plainly visible, as they take every opportunity to imitate the character." And not only juveniles imitated the pose, the pugnacity, the obvious toughness of this fireman.

Moses Humphreys' downfall was sudden and terrible. His company and Engine Company No. 15 had a furious fight upon returning from a fire, and he was rendered senseless by a brother of the actor who had made this bully boy so famous. Moses could not live down this disgrace. He at once set out for the South Seas, and it was rumored that he became the fire chief of the Sandwich

A New York Race Two pumpers rush in frantic rivalry to the burning of the Crystal Palace in New York. This is one of a series of lithographs by Thomas & Wylie entitled "Firemen, Past and Present." *Library of Congress*

Islands. But after his departure, his feats lived on, with embellishments. He was Paul Bunyan in a fireman's red shirt, and every smoke-eater longed at times to be just like him.

Some brawls arose when street loafers resented the vaunted physical superiority of the firemen, and smoke-eaters and their equipment were sometimes the victims of sheer vandalism. In Philadelphia, there were fights between Catholic and Prottestant fire companies. In Boston, a company that took in newly arrived immigrants was apt to be pummeled by superpatriotic nativists. In some communities, when firemen appeared to be getting too strongly entrenched politically, "other interests" would incite riots, so that one or more companies would be disbanded for fighting.

But most fights were for the sheer joy of fighting;

strong, proud, well-muscled men wanted an opportunity to enjoy physical conflict. In 1853, a Philadelphia pamphlet reported: "Pastime and Pleasure.— Having occasion to walk out Walnut street, yesterday, about noon, when about half way between Fourth and Fifth streets, two of our independent fire companies, on their road home, came in collision. The weather being exceedingly raw and disagreeable, and withal cold, doubtless the members thought it a fine opportunity to indulge in their almost daily sport, and at the same time promote respiration and keep up their very honorable character. The battle raged for a time with terrible fury. . . . Every comatable missile was put in requisition, and every effort was made for a glorious victory."

More than anything else, it was excess rowdy-

Fighting Firemen (*Opposite*) This lithograph, made in 1848, shows a scene from a play about a New York fireman. The character representing Mose (a genuine smoke-eater) is persuasively "arguing" that the hose line of a rival company should be removed from a hydrant that he wishes to use. *Museum of the City of New York*

Which Man Do You Want to Take On? Gaze into the faces of the men of Washington Hose Company of New York and decide where an "easy" man is. Then imagine how it would be to engage in a brawl with all twelve of these firemen. Rollo, the dog, was no slouch as a fighter, either. *H. V. Smith Museum of the Home Insurance Company*

A Rough Fire in Philadelphia Here is a $400,000 fire at North and Commerce Streets in Philadelphia on May 1, 1856. The fire started in a rag and paper warehouse, but the blaze soon roared out of control and a general alarm was sounded, to which every company in the city responded. According to a contemporary account, "Strange as it may seem, at the very height of the conflagration two fire companies got into a quarrel, and a young man was stabbed in the right breast, and conveyed to a hospital, supposed to be in a dying condition." The fatality was unusual; the "quarrel" was not.

ism that brought about the knell of the volunteer fire departments in the larger cities. Henry Ward Beecher asked if the critics would have a company of French dancing masters to extinguish fires; it was well, he declared, that we had rough, strong men to war against the flames. But he was in a minority. It was generally believed that this rowdyism was only one symptom that discipline was lacking. And discipline, it was felt, required a professional fire department, under authority.

Even in 1858, when few departments were professional, one reporter felt that firemen were not so bad as painted. "From a careful investigation, it will be found that the firemen as a body will average, in point of respectability and worth, as producers and artisans, in point of moral character as citizens, and indeed in all the relations of life,

equal to any organized class of men. In morals they are above the military." Thirty years later, in nostalgic retrospect, another writer declared: "Take them all in all, they were brave men, devoted men —we shall never look upon their likes again."

PITTSBURGH'S FIRE OF 1845

Even the most factional of fire departments forgot about company lines and rivalries when the tocsin sounded for a serious blaze. The brawling smoke-eaters of Pittsburgh, Pennsylvania, were a case in point. That community saw its first volunteer fire company in 1793. The competitive aggressiveness of the early firemen brought about a constantly increasing number of rival companies, and by 1845 this curious situation existed: there were more firemen available for duty than could be serviced by the local water supply. There were too many firemen. Or, stated differently, there was not enough water. In either case, all of the firemen could not work at the same time.

On April 10, 1845, a woman kindled an open fire to heat water in order to wash some clothing. A strong wind was blowing, and sparks were carried to a near-by icehouse, which was ignited. Whirling breezes carried burning straw to a frame building, which was soon in flames. Next to be destroyed were a cotton factory, a church, a bank, a newspaper publishing plant, the quarters of Vigilant Fire Company, a bookstore, a bindery. After that, no recital of losses is possible. There was chaos.

The city was largely of wood, which had become dried after a two weeks' absence of rain. In the lower town, there were only two water mains, both small. The reservoir was low.

The rapid advance of the flames prevented the salvage of much property; some merchandise burned in the streets after it had been pulled out of business establishments at great personal hazard.

Structures burned, said a witness, "as quick as a flash of powder." Zinc roofs melted and ran down rain spouts because of the heat. Another witness, who was to become the father of Andrew Mellon, recalled how excited householders threw china and crockery from the upper floors of their homes.

Firemen battled desperately against increasingly heavy odds. One of their helpers was a grimy-faced boy named Stephen Foster.

Gunpowder was used in an attempt to halt the flames, but the fire only burned itself out when it ran out of fuel. Some fifty-six acres were ravaged by the conflagration, about one thousand buildings being destroyed. One-third of the city was in ashes; two-thirds of the wealth had been destroyed. There were twelve thousand homeless persons. "Merchants, mechanics, workingmen, all, all were ruined." Losses were estimated to be about ten million dollars, but contributions came from sympathizers throughout the nation. From Paris, the Rothschild family sent aid. Only two persons were lost in the holocaust.

VIEW of the RUINS of the CITY of PITTSBURGH from BOYD'S HILL.

The Pittsburgh Fire W. C. Wail made this painting of the Great Fire of 1849. Wagner & McGuignan prepared the lithograph. *Library of Congress*

Muscles and Courage

and Steam

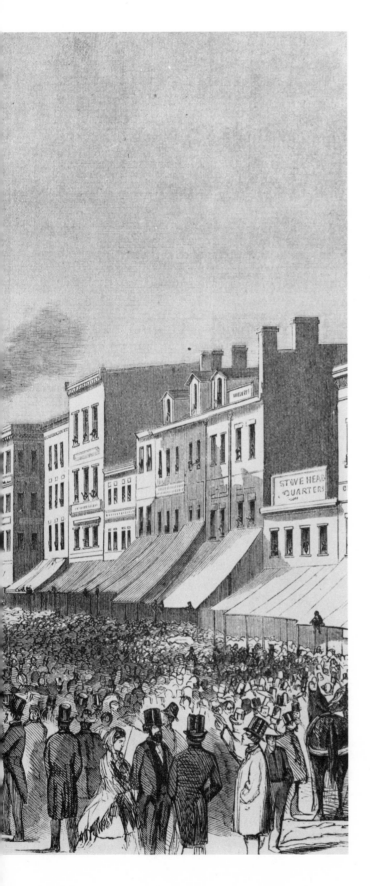

The invention of the steam fire engine in England in 1828 left American firemen cold. Their apparatus and techniques extinguished fires; what more could one want?

But the London fire insurance companies were delighted with the new fire engine, and they awarded the inventors the magnificent sum of five pounds. The steamer was of ten horsepower, with two horizontal cylinders and pumps, and it could throw from thirty to fifty tons of water per hour to a height of ninety feet. The designers were Ericcson and Braithwaite. At the burning of the Argyle Rooms in 1829, one newspaper said of the steamer, "For the first time, fire was extinguished by the mechanical power of fire." Six steamers were in use in London by 1842.

In 1840, one of the codesigners, John Ericcson, came to the United States, where his inventive genius was to turn out such marvels as the screw propeller and the primitive ironclad U.S.S. *Monitor* (of *Monitor* and *Merrimac* fame). He promptly won a gold medal that had been offered by the Mechanics' Institute of New York (after a bad fire) for a successful steam fire engine. His winning entry was a design for a machine that could get up steam in ten minutes and had the power of 108 men, with a stream of water that could be projected into the air to a height of 105 feet.

Ericcson's design remained on paper, and it was Paul Rapsey Hodge of New York who built the first American steamer in 1840–41. The pump could throw a stream of water to a height of 166 feet through a $2\frac{1}{8}$-inch nozzle. It was so heavy (almost eight tons) and clumsy that, while two horses could pull the machine on a plane surface, hills were beyond equine aid. Accordingly, the

A Steamer Contest When the Ohio & Mississippi Railroad depot was opened in Cincinnati in 1857, the various steamers in the fire department engaged in a contest of their own. Wrote an eye-witness: "The glistening drops sparkled like so many diamonds in the air, and the vast crowd assembled gave expression to their admiration by stentorian *vivas.*"

steamer had to be converted to a self-propeller. Hodge attempted to interest the insurance companies in his engine, but there was little enthusiasm. Firemen simply wanted to have nothing to do with the monstrosity, although Pearl Hose Company No. 28 of New York tried it for a few months. The engine was named "Exterminator."

Resistance to the Industrial Revolution occurred in almost every walk of life, but the volunteer firemen were perhaps the last holdouts. The smoke-eaters could see a threat to their way of life. Thus their resistance was bottomed on more than religious, financial, and safety grounds. The influence of the firemen upon public officials postponed adoption of the steamers long after their practi-

cality had been demonstrated. Didn't America become great because of its muscles and courage, demanded the firemen. Let's keep it the same way. Where men aren't strong enough, or long-winded enough, there may be need for artificial substitutes for human brawn; but that is not the situation which we have in America. Them with muscles, use 'em. And the public at large was willing to accept this pronouncement. The firemen were too politically potent to antagonize. And they became more numerous, more boisterous every day. It was this rowdyism that brought about their own undoing at the hands of the steamer.

In 1851, an unusually fierce battle occurred between two Cincinnati companies, Western Hose

An Early Steamer Advertisement This is an advertising poster used by A. B. & E. Latta of Cincinnati to proclaim the merits of its early steamer. Note its name: "Lightning." *New-York Historical Society*

The First American-Built Steamer This engine had horizontal cylinders and pumps, a locomotive boiler, and wrought iron wheels. Its resemblance to its progenitors (railroad engines) is obvious.

Company No. 3 and Washington Company No. 1. They met at Augusta and John streets en route to a fire; and before the issue was settled with fists, ten companies were involved. From across the river the Covington, Kentucky, Fire Company rushed, not to help extinguish the fire, but to aid the Washington boys in their time of need. Meanwhile the fire did not wait and a planing mill was completely destroyed. The mayor himself was unable to restore order.

At this juncture, the advocates of law and order demanded a change. It was obvious that the volunteer companies had passed into the control of the worst elements in town. Firehouses had become clubhouses for organized ruffianism. Cincinnati's chief engineer set out to find a way to extinguish fires without so much manual labor. To show that fire engines could be worked independently of the rowdy element, he helped to finance the invention of a local manufacturer named Moses Latta. The inventor soon complained that spies sent by the volunteer firemen were prying into his work and that he had been threatened with bodily

injury unless he announced that the steamer was an impossibility.

The Latta family contained several mechanical geniuses who had developed locomotives, planing machines, and other heavy equipment. Their fire steamer was set on three wheels, the foremost of which was used for steering. The piston rods of the steam cylinders were continued to form the rods of the pumps; when required, these rods also could be coupled to the driving wheels. From one to six streams of water could be thrown, with a total capacity of up to two thousand barrels of water per hour. The steamer could get to work in five minutes, but four men and four horses were required to get the machine out of its house.

"We claim to be the *original* and first *projectors* of the *first successful Steam Fire Engine* in the world's history," the Lattas were to declare in 1860. "There have been many attempts at making a machine of such construction as would answer to extinguish fires; but none of them proved to be available in a sufficiently short space of time to warrant their use as a Fire Apparatus."

The arithmetic was all in favor of the steamer. If the new engine could take the place of twelve hand pumpers, and if each hand pumper had from fifty to seventy-five firemen and runners attached to it, it was obvious that a considerable amount of excess manpower could be eliminated at every fire. Fewer firehouses would be needed.

The Cincinnati City Council decided to take the big step. When a professional department of a reasonable number of trained men was proposed, the enraged volunteers invaded the council chamber and threatened physical injury to those who sought to legislate the "vamps" out of existence. The councilmen timidly explained that they had just purchased the new Latta steamer and that to place such a delicate instrument in the hands of unskilled volunteers would be useless. The paid department was authorized. This was the first professional fire department in the United States and the first department to use steamers in extinguishing fires. The new department was inaugurated on April 1, 1853.

As chief there was named Miles Greenwood, a machine shop operator who had been one of the most forceful of the dissenting volunteers. (He was to turn over his compensation to the Mechanics' Institute.)

The first fire to which the paid department was summoned was on Sycamore Street above Fourth. Let the first driver recount his adventures: "There the engine stood, steam up, four large gray horses hitched to it, a crowd looking at it, and Greenwood as mad as the devil because he couldn't get a man to drive the horses. You see all the firemen were opposed to this new invention because they believed it would spoil their fun, and nobody wanted to be stoned by them, and then the horses were kicking about so that everybody was afraid on that account. My brother says: 'Larry, you can drive those horses I know.' And Greenwood said: 'If you can drive them I wish you would; I'll pay you for it.' My business was teaming, you see. And just as I was with my Sunday clothes on, I jumped on the back of a wheel horse, seized the rein, spoke to the horses, and out we went kiting. Miles Greenwood went ahead, telling the people to get out of the way—the streets were full of people."

According to one account: "Then down came the

An 1856 Cincinnati Fire Three steamers are working at this blaze. At the extreme left may be noted a 4-horse hitch that has been taken from one of the engines; no doubt the animals would have become restive if they had to stand next to the snorting, wheezing, palpitating pumper for long.

Cincinnati's First Steamer This picture appeared in the Annual Report of the Chief Engineer of the Cincinnati Fire Department in 1854. It is difficult to see in this monstrosity the delightfully graceful steamer that was shortly to be developed.

A Procession An early 3-wheeled Cincinnati steamer responds to an alarm. Four horses pull the ponderous mechanism, and two "outriders" help to negotiate the turns.

Horse Drawn Hose Reel After Cincinnati acquired its first steamer, other equipment was re-designed for maximum efficiency to match the engine. This photograph shows the hose cart in use in about 1853. *Historical and Philosophical Society of Ohio*

An Early Steamer Fire House The first steamers could not be stored in conventional fire houses. Instead, huge structures had to be constructed. This is the house of the Fourth District Steam Fire Engine in Cincinnati. Note the shaft and other equipment for hitching horses to this Latta steamer. *Historical and Philosophical Society of Ohio*

Horses Take Over Here is an early effort to achieve what was to become the most glorious of fire institutions, the horse-drawn steamer. This picture appeared in the Annual Report of the Chief Engineer of the Cincinnati Fire Department in 1860.

great steam fire-engine, four mammoth gray horses in front of it, at a gallop; the smoke streaming from its stack, the fire flashing from its grates. Its ponderous wheels ground the cobblestones into powder as they struck them; and as the great monster went down the hill, people woke as out of a trance and started after it. The engine was brought in front of the block and soon afterward stream after stream shot from it. The houses were among the most valuable in the city, and were stored with costly goods. The time had come; the engine was there. Four streams had been thrown when the cry, 'The hose is cut,' rang out. Then the melée began."

The huge crowd was not merely curious. The displaced volunteers were there to destroy the engine and to disable the paid firemen. But Chief Greenwood thoughtfully had summoned the skilled fighters in his foundry, and no hostile hand could be laid on the "sham squirt," as the volunteers derisively had named the huge pumper. The new order had been vindicated and defended.

In the First Annual Report of the chief engineer

of the Cincinnati Fire Department in 1854, the real reason for the introduction of the steamer was not overlooked. "Under the present control the Engine Houses are no longer nurseries where the youth of the city are trained in vice, vulgarity and debauchery, and where licentiousness holds his nightly revels. The Sabbath day is no longer desecrated by the yells and fierce conflicts of rival Fire Companies, who sought the occasion offered by false alarms, often gotten up for the purpose of making brutal assaults upon each other; our citizens, male and female, pass our Engine Houses without being insulted by the coarse vulgarities of the persons collected around them."

Cincinnati's first steamer, "Uncle Joe Ross," had many mechanical shortcomings, but the city was not prepared to pay for another steamer just yet. The president of the Chamber of Commerce advanced a generous check for a new pumper, and public-spirited citizens quickly added their contributions. The funds provided for the cost of a new model, which was appropriately named "Citizens' Gift."

A. B: LATTA'S
STEAM FIRE ENGINE.

Cincinnati's Second Steamer "Citizens' Gift" was an improved model that had been designed to correct the faults of "Uncle Joe Ross." A fire signal tower is in the background. *Historical and Philosophical Society of Ohio*

A Steamer Blows Up Here is the horrible explosion of a Cincinnati steamer in 1855. A trial was being held before a committee from the Chicago City Council when the boiler blew up, with the resultant death of one fireman and injuries to others.

The city continued to buy new steamers. Municipal representatives from other parts of the nation came to see the innovation. In 1855, during a demonstration for the Chicago City Council, the "Uncle Joe Ross" blew up, killing one fireman, two spectators, and injuring others.

But Greenwood lost none of his enthusiasm. The steamer, he declared, was the only fireman that never threw brickbats and that never got drunk. Its only fault was that it could note vote.

By 1860, Cincinnati had eight steamers in service, with only three active hand pumpers in the city proper. The chief engineer reported in that year that "it is time that steam, which is cheaper, be substituted for bone and muscle."

"The Steamer!
We'll Ever Adore You...."

Cincinnati's sponsorship of the first practical American steam fire engine was not duplicated nationally with either speed or enthusiasm. It was not only the men in the ranks who had their doubts. Officers also mistrusted the machine.

In 1855, New York saw its first working steamers. A manufacturer, Lee & Larned, furnished two steamers to the city, but the firemen at first would have nothing to do with this equipment. A delegation of volunteers petitioned the City Council to reject the machines. On February 9, a contest was held in City Hall Park between one of the newfangled steamers and a tremendous hand pumper of the type known as a "man-killer." The latter stream was slightly the longer, and most of the firemen shouted happily: human muscles were better than a machine. But two fire department officials noted that whereas the exhausted firemen dropped at the brakes, the steamer steadily pumped its water. "John, that stream stays there," commented one officer. "Yes, it does." "Well, that settles it."

But New York was not yet ready to accept such a verdict. When Valley Forge Engine Company No. 46 acquired a steamer, its crew was warned by other firemen that the engine would certainly

New York's First Steamer
Parking the engine was only one of the problems.

be taken away from them and dumped into the river. Even the chief engineer of the fire department looked upon the steamers with suspicion, and in his 1859 report he stated that they pumped too much water and there would be "more damage by that element than the one it is sought to subdue. The propriety of their introduction into general use is questionable."

By 1860, New York had a new chief engineer, who declared in his annual report for that year: "There is no doubt but that these engines, at large fires, are of service as an auxiliary to the hand engines; but, in my judgment, they can never take the place of the hand apparatus."

New Orleans obtained its first steamer in 1855, the same year as New York's first practical machine. This was a Latta pumper, the "Young America," that had been purchased by the city's fire insurance underwriters. But the Annual Report of the chief engineer in 1858 showed unmistakably that this newfangled equipment was not here to stay: "And while on this subject, I may be permitted to state that that costly and expensive piece of machinery has, in my opinion, totally failed to perform anything like proportionate service to the amount of money annually expended on it by the contractor, say six thousand dollars. I am ready to admit that, when once at work, its performances are excellent and lasting, but the opportunities to get to work are 'few and far between.' The whole apparatus is too heavy, its weight being over eighteen thousand pounds, together with the alluvial state of our soil and the bad state of our streets, it may readily be judged with what dispatch, if at all, it can be brought to a conflagration. . . . [F]ew wharves are able to sustain themselves under its crushing weight. . . . These, Gentlemen, are the principal reasons why the sanguine anticipations of the original advocates of this great 'Fire Annihilator' have not been realized, and were it not for

Crescent City Equipment Steam engine and tender of Eagle Company No. 7 in New Orleans in 1868.

Family Resemblance (above) Firemen rarely look like their engines today; but there seems to be a very strong resemblance between these and their steamer. This engine was used by a Philadelphia company in about 1865. These volunteer firemen appear to have been men of substance. *Historical Society of Pennsylvania*

Union League Fire (below) The burning of the Union League Building in Philadelphia in 1866 was the occasion of this heroic rescue of the flag. The firemen must have done a good job on the building, too, for the structure today looks just the same as it did ninety years ago.

COMMITTEE to put the STEAM ENGINE in Service
GEº F. GORDON *Chairman* : – O. H. P. PARKER J. K. KNORR M. D. W. M. PARHAM
BUILDER of the ENGINE
A SHAWK. – CINCINNATI

Philadelphia's First Steamer   In 1855, a group of Philadelphians acquired this machine from Abel Shawk of Cincinnati, for a time a partner of Latta.

the promptness of the hand engines, and the fact that there are six more in service than contemplated by the ordinance, the fallacy of their hopes would have been sadly illustrated in various instances ere this."

In 1855, Philadelphia received its first steamer. As the city was financially embarrassed at the time, a group of citizens purchased the pumper for $9,500 from A. Shawk of Cincinnati, a former partner of the Lattas. A Committee on Trust and Fire Department took title to the machine. For some time a dispute raged as to what should be done with the equipment. The committee was disinclined

to turn the engine over to a volunteer company which mistrusted it. And there was even dispute as to which fires the steamer should be brought, for the city authorities wanted the pumper to go only to large conflagrations. As a public service, the committee published a report of its trials and tribulations. "It is not intended to give in this report a history of the intense opposition and hatred manifested against the steam engine," it is stated in the *Report of the Sub-Committee To Put The Steam Fire Engine 'Young America' In Service.*

But by 1858, steamers had passed their baptism of fire in Philadelphia. In that year, the celebrated Hibernia Fire Engine Company No. 1 acquired a new engine, and the experienced smoke-eaters of this company became enthusiastic rather than merely tolerant about the steamer. They took it with them to tournaments throughout the East and no doubt were instrumental in popularizing the steamer among firemen.

Steam Against Muscle (*Opposite*) The first contest between machine and man was won by the latter in 1855. But the machine's greater staying power was to prove decisive.

83

The steamer was introduced in Boston in 1854. "It was long regarded as a failure," recorded one writer twenty-seven years later, "and the firemen found the English language quite insufficient to express the contempt they felt for it." The Annual Report of the chief engineer in 1856 declared: "The past year, the Steam Fire Engine, Miles Greenwood, has been brought into service three times, but has not given me that satisfaction I should wish." But the 1858 report reflected a great change of heart. "The subject of introducing Steam Fire Engines into the Department has been constantly before the public during the year, and there is no question now of their great superiority over all hand machines." By 1860, Boston had banished all manual apparatus to the rural districts. On very rare occasions was it recalled.

Louisville, Kentucky, established its Steam Fire Department in 1858. Here the authorities were enthusiastic from the start. The First Annual Report of the chief engineer in 1859 declared: "The fires have not only been fewer and losses smaller, but the alarms have been less frequent—and thus are avoided the riotings and shedding of blood which have been attendant upon fire alarms, while the volunteer system was in existence—and some of these alarms, it was supposed, and not without cause, were raised for the express purpose of bringing about hostile meetings between some of the companies."

In 1888, a New Jersey writer noted that "the volunteer firemen of Paterson in common with firemen everywhere bitterly opposed the introduction of steam fire engines. They looked upon it [sic] as the death knell of the volunteer system, hence they looked upon it with anything but feelings of satisfaction." But in 1860, after they had seen tests at Poughkeepsie, New York, a group of Paterson's volunteers petitioned the Board of Aldermen to procure a steamer. A committee of aldermen refused the request, reporting "that steam fire engines were as yet an experiment and none of the committee had ever seen one of them in operation."

By 1860, steel and brass were used instead of cast iron in the manufacture of steamers, and a noticeable change in size, shape, and weight took place. The nine-ton monsters were replaced by relatively delicate machines that could be drawn by men.

Mechanical Ingenuity The steamer's piston wheel was fastened with a chain to the rear wheels of this engine, and horses were eliminated. The apparatus' speed was not very considerable, and the firemen do not seem to be afraid of being run over by this New York City engine.

STEAM FIRE ENGINE LITTLE GIANT Nº 6.
ORGANIZED FEBRUARY 14TH 1860, CHICAGO ILL.

Little Giant This Edward Mendel lithograph depicts an engine built by the Amoskeag Manufacturing Company of Manchester, New Hampshire. *Chicago Historical Society*

The early steamers bore individual names, as the hand pumpers had borne. Even as late as the Great Chicago Fire of 1871, the officials referred to their pumpers by names rather than company numbers. But the real proof that the steamer had arrived was furnished by a poem in the *Firemen's Herald* in 1882, which contained these touching words:

The Steamer! We'll ever adore you. . . .

BARNUM'S MUSEUM

Some firemen, who could not *imagine* how a steamer could be more effective than manpower, had to be shown. Many of New York's smoke-eaters had such a demonstration at one of the city's first great fires since the introduction of the steamer. This was the burning of Barnum's Museum.

85

A Hand-Drawn Steamer (above) Just as though they still had a hand pumper, these men may still run with their engine.

Barnum's Museum (below) Depicted is the fire on July 13, 1865. *National Board of Fire Underwriters*

GERMAN AMERICAN

BURNING OF BARNUM'S MUSEUM, JULY 13TH 1865.
AFTER THE ORIGINAL PAINTING BY C.P. CRANCH, IN POSSESSION OF THE GERMAN AMERICAN INSURANCE CO. NEW YORK.

Engine Company No 10, Chicago This photograph was taken about ten years after the Civil War, but the poses of the men are reminiscent of group pictures of soldiers. The booted men look ready, in the words of the Civil War song, to "Jine the Cavalry." *Illinois State Historical Library*

New York's First Horse-Drawn Steamer Metropolitan Steam Fire Engine Company No. 1 was organized on July 31, 1865. The apparatus shown is an Amoskeag steamer, built that same year; the pump was of the piston type.

Phineas T. Barnum, that greatest of showmen, often declared that a sucker was born every minute. When it came to fires, Barnum was that sucker. On four different occasions, major fires ravaged his places of business.

Barnum's American Museum, which for reasons that quickly will appear was obliged to occupy a number of different premises in New York City, was a vast and unique establishment. Live animals, birds, and great sea beasts competed for public attention with bizarre human beings, unkindly but effectively advertised as "freaks." Curiosities and rarities of all sorts were on display.

On July 13, 1865, the American Museum was located at the corner of Ann Street and Broadway, just south of City Hall Park. A fire broke out at the noon hour, at a time when the building was almost empty. That was fortunate, for the crowds of patrons were sometimes unmanageably large. Volunteer firemen rescued the staff and performers, not without difficulty in some cases; the Fat Lady presented some tough technical problems, as did the Giantess. It was reported in the press (that ubiquitous Barnum!) that several firemen were smitten with the woolly-headed Albino Woman. Harmless animals were released by the firemen; the more dangerous beasts could not be freed. One smoke-eater engaged in a life-and-death struggle on the street with a Bengal tiger; his ax was equal to the emergency. Birds were freed from their confinement, and for some time subsequently townspeople wondered at the strange plumage of certain winged creatures they encountered. Half a million dollars' worth of property was destroyed. The steamer "John G. Storm" was credited with having saved $250,000 worth of property.

Other fires at the respective Barnum's Museum were on November 25, 1864, when Confederate agents fired the structure as one of a series of simultaneous blazes set in New York; on March 3, 1868; and on December 24, 1872. After this dismal record, Barnum could have had few rarities in his museum more unusual than a fire insurance policy issued upon his premises.

A New York Steamer Explodes   On the night of June 18, 1868, Engine Company No. 1 of the new New York professional fire department was pumping at a fire, when the boiler exploded. At that moment, the Old Bowery Theatre was just letting out and the street was crowded. Five persons were killed and twenty-two were injured. An investigation disclosed that the steamer's safety valve had been strapped down.

Hand-Drawn Steamer   This W. M. Aker steamer is of a very early type. Unlike the first monstrosities, this apparatus is light in weight and horses were not required for its propulsion. *Western Reserve Historical Society*

The Willard Hotel Fire When Willard's Hotel in Washington caught fire on May 9, 1861, the blaze was seen by Colonel Ellsworth's Fire Zouaves, who were bivouacked in the Capitol. His troops had been recruited entirely from New York's volunteer smoke-eaters. The colonel ordered that one hundred men attend to the blaze; but the entire regiment leaped from the Capitol windows. The efforts of these highly trained men were spectacular, but a reporter was more impressed by something quite different. "They destroyed nothing unnecessarily," he wrote, "and nothing was missing."

The Civil War

No one knows just where the Civil War started. Perhaps it had its beginning in a firehouse.

In 1859, John Brown attempted to liberate the slaves in Virginia. With seventeen men, he thought to start a movement that would be joined by all the slaves as well as by the friends of liberty. But when United States troops, under the command of Robert E. Lee, were sent to Harpers Ferry to put down the insurrection, Brown's little force took refuge in a firehouse. "The building in which the insurgents had made their stand was the fire-engine house," noted the New York *Tribune* of October 16, "and no doubt the most defensible building in the armory." Some of the first bloodshed in "the war to free the slaves" took place in this firehouse. Brown was captured beside a hand pumper bearing the proud words, "Old Rough and Ready." Half a century earlier, Thomas Jefferson had said that slavery frightened him like a fire bell in the night; it was thus appropriate that the first armed conflict over the slavery issue in Virginia centered around a firehouse.

When the war broke out, firemen were among the most enthusiastic recruits. In New York, every firehouse became a recruiting station, and a crack regiment was quickly formed. The Eleventh New York was its official name, but no one called it anything but the First Fire Zouaves. All of the men were New York firemen, as were all of the officers except for Colonel Ellsworth. When the regiment was temporarily stationed in Washington, the men took over from the undermanned local firemen the task of saving Willard's Hotel from the flames.

Abraham Lincoln Reports a Fire

One of Lincoln's first appearances on the national scene took place in 1848, when he delivered a subcommittee report to the House of Representatives. The report concerned the premises of a postmaster that had been destroyed by fire.

After the first Battle of Bull Run, the men of this regiment captured a trophy more dear to them than any Confederate flag; they seized the pumper of Valley Forge Engine Company No. 1 of Alexandria, Virginia. For many years after the war, this engine was used by a New York fire company.

In 1862, the Secretary of War requested the mayor of New York to send an experienced fireman to Fortress Monroe, Virginia, to organize a fire

THIRTIETH CONGRESS—FIRST SESSION.

Report No. 326.

[To accompany H. R. Joint Resolution, 18.]

HOUSE OF REPRESENTATIVES.

H. M. BARNEY.

MARCH 9, 1848.

Mr. LINCOLN, from the Committee on the Post Office and Post Roads, made the following

REPORT:

The Committee on the Post Office and Post Roads, to whom was referred the petition of H. M. Barney, postmaster at Brimfield, Peoria county, Illinois, report:

That they have been satisfied by evidence, that on the 15th of December, 1847, said petitioner had his store, with some fifteen hundred dollars worth of goods, together with all the papers of the post office, entirely destroyed by fire; and that the specie funds of the office were melted down, partially lost, and partially destroyed; that his large individual loss entirely precludes the idea of embezzlement; that the balances due the department of former quarters has been only about twenty-five dollars; and that owing to the destruction of the papers, the exact amount due for the quarter ending December 31st, 1847, cannot be ascertained. They therefore report a joint resolution, releasing said petitioner from paying anything for the quarter last mentioned.

John Brown and the Firehouse The interior of the firehouse where Brown holed up to resist arrest. In addition to a hose reel, there may be noted on a hand pumper the proud words, "Old Rough and Ready."

department there. John Baulch, a veteran New York smoke-eater, was given the assignment; he had not missed a major fire since 1835, and he had risen through the ranks to the position of assistant chief engineer of the volunteer fire department. When the Confederate ironclad *Virginia* (better known by its prewar name of *Merrimac*) menaced Fortress Monroe, Chief Baulch requisitioned fire engines from Philadelphia and Baltimore. He was next appointed chief engineer of the army's Division of the South, where his duty was to follow the advancing troops and to take charge of all fire apparatus in Southern communities occupied by Federal troops. If no other men were available to serve, he organized fire companies with soldiers for the protection of occupied communities.

When the Northern troops captured New Orleans, General Benjamin F. Butler became military commander of the city. He required all of the citizens (including clergymen) to take an oath of allegiance to the United States. The only exception was made in the case of the volunteer firemen, who refused to protect the city from fire unless they would be relieved of the hated oath. Butler, who declined to capitulate to ministers and to physicians, was obliged to yield to the firemen.

The bloodiest uprising ever known in the United States occurred in the New York Draft Riots of July, 1863, and volunteer firemen were both the villains and the heroes of this event. They were the villains because they triggered the revolt (although if they had not done so, someone else unquestionably would have). They were the heroes because of their deeds in restoring order and in saving life.

There had been much opposition to the first conscription act, which seemed to savor of Old World despotism rather than of democracy. But on July 11, 1863, the draft began in New York. Various enrollment offices were set up under the direction of provost marshals, who gathered the names of eligible men in their districts. Each marshal threw the available names in a spinning wheel in his own office, and the names were drawn, lottery-fashion, by a blindfolded person. On July 13, the name of an officer of Black Joke Engine Company No. 33 was drawn from the wheel, but some of his faithful firemen took direct action to see that the name was not recorded. They used the weapon that they best understood: fire. The draft office was quickly given to the flames.

Word spread rapidly to thousands of other persons who were congregated in front of the remaining draft offices, and the scene was generally repeated. When the volunteer firemen arrived to extinguish the flames, they were set upon by mobs who wanted no extinguishment. Then the rioters got completely out of hand. Police were virtually helpless in fighting hordes that pillaged saloons, stores, and armories (for arms). The city was almost denuded of troops; this was only a week after the Battle of Gettysburg.

Next the mob turned its fury upon colored people; wasn't this draft to supply cannon fodder for a war that colored people somehow had occasioned? Negroes on the streets were beaten up and sometimes lynched; hotels and other places of business that employed Negroes were invaded and burned.

The Evacuation of Richmond   This Currier & Ives lithograph shows the evacuation of the Confederate capital just before the fall of the city. *National Board of Fire Underwriters*

ED BY CURRIER &IVES   Entered according to Act of Congress AD 1865, by Currier & Ives, in the Clerks Office of the District Court of the United States for the Southern Dist of N Y   125 NASSAU ST NEW YORK

THE EVACUATION OF RICHMOND VA.

BY THE GOVERNMENT OF THE SOUTHERN CONFEDERACY ON THE NIGHT OF APRIL 2ND 1865

The New York Draft Riots

No firemen are visible at the scene of the burning of the Colored Orphan Asylum during New York's terrible Draft Riots in 1863. That absence was forcible; the firemen were not allowed by the rioters to ex-

tinguish the blaze. The treatment received by the little colored children may be seen in a number of episodes in this picture; even white children participated in the assaults.

The Orphan Asylum for Colored Children occupied a spacious tract on the east side of Fifth Avenue, between Forty-third and Forty-fourth streets. Two hundred children were safely evacuated before a torch-bearing mob arrived, but the building was fired anyway. When the firemen arrived to extinguish the blaze, they were ferociously attacked, and Chief Engineer John Decker was seized by the rioters. A rope was tied around his neck; the fire department almost lost one of its greatest heroes. "Gentlemen," exclaimed Decker calmly, "do you think you can stop the government's draft by stopping mine?" The pun was successful, and he was released.

For three more days, the mob pillaged the city almost at will. The exhausted police were helped by numerous volunteer firemen, who patrolled the streets and broke up mobs. Then troops arrived from Gettysburg, and order was restored. Meanwhile, five million dollars in property damage was sustained, with twelve hundred buildings burned and twice that many damaged. Perhaps 2,500 persons were killed, and three or four times that number were injured.

There was much fire damage incidental to the fighting. Thus before Pickett could begin his great charge at Gettysburg, he ordered the burning of the Codori farmhouse, which was in his line of march. There was also some malicious burning of the property of prominent persons on the opposing side. The first chairman of the powerful congressional Reconstruction Committee after the war was the vindictive Representative Thad Stevens of Pennsylvania, and many historians believe that he treated the South so harshly because the Confederates wantonly had burned his iron foundry near Chambersburg. Such destruction usually brought reciprocity. When the Confederates needlessly burned the home of the Northern Postmaster General in Maryland, the Federal troops quickly retaliated by giving the torch to the house of a former Confederate Secretary of War. When the Southern General Pickett outmaneuvered General Butler at Petersburg, the latter retaliated by burning the Pickett ancestral home on Turkey Island, Virginia.

The Burning of Columbia, S. C.

Who was responsible for the burning of this capital city cannot be said. The Northern general Sherman claimed that the retreating Confederates had fired bales of cotton that were piled in the streets and that a high wind made the flames impossible to quench. Others claimed that the fires had been started by escaped

Federal prisoners before the city fell. But Southerners declared that Sherman's advance cavalry, under General Kilpatrick ("Kill Cavalry") had set the fires. One Southerner wrote that the scene "would have driven Alaric the Goth into frenzied ecstasies." This illustration is by William Waud.

Several large-scale fires were even more atrocious. Several communities were given ultimatums by invading armies: unless you pay a specified ransom, your town will be burned down. Chambersburg, Pennsylvania, was razed when the ransom could not be obtained for the Confederate General Early.

During the war, a pro-Southern movement known as the Copperheads sprang up in various Northern states, including Pennsylvania. One such group, the Heidelberg Brigade, tried to set fire to a prison in Reading in order to free the prisoners; but when the Junior Fire Company responded with its engine, the insurgent leader mistook the brass nozzle for artillery. "*Do cumpt de cannon; spring, bouver, spring!* (Here comes the cannon; jump, boys, jump!)" he called to his Pennsylvania Dutch followers. That was the end of this uprising.

On the evening of November 25, 1864, Confederate secret agents tried to terrorize New York by setting a series of simultaneous fires. Eleven hotels, Barnum's Museum, and two theaters were set on fire. But the volunteer firemen were so quick and efficient that the damage was small, and the citizens refused to become demoralized according to plan.

Far more damage was caused by General Sherman's raiders, who had the definite assignment of making the South sue for peace by undermining home-front morale. These troops destroyed everything in their path; even today, Sherman is usually associated with the phrase, "War is Hell." This was the first modern example of the concept of "total warfare" that exists today. But Sherman always maintained stoutly that the burning of Charleston, South Carolina, after its capture by his troops was an accident rather than design.

The greatest fire loss of the war was self-inflicted. When the Confederates discovered in April, 1865, that they could no longer defend Richmond, they set fire to the huge government tobacco and other warehouses. The flames soon reached the streets, which were flooded with whisky from barrels that had been destroyed by government order, and a large part of the capital was utterly destroyed. Firemen were helpless as rioters, hoping to profit from the disorder after the Southern soldiers de-

Reconciliation This handsome hose reel was sent by the firemen of New York to their compatriots in Columbia, South Carolina, to replace apparatus that had been lost during the Civil War.

Civil War Fire Engines (above) Such equipment was rarely photographed against a military background, for the photographers were more interested in martial paraphernalia. This scene shows the Employees' Hospital and firehouse at an army installation in Chattanooga, Tennessee. *National Archives*

Army Fire Chief (below) John Baulch was chief of the fire department of the Southern division of the Federal army during the Civil War. *Fort Monroe Museum*

parted, cut the hose. By one of war's paradoxes, the invading Northern army saved the enemy capital from total destruction by extinguishing the fires set by the Confederates.

The final fire chapter of the Civil War, a sort of sequel, is more pleasant to relate. Two years after the war's end, Independence Hose Company No. 1 of Charleston, South Carolina, made an appeal to the North for old hose and cast-off apparatus, to replace what had been lost in the city's great fire. The firemen of New York personally raised five thousand dollars with which they purchased a new silver-mounted hose carriage. The engine was shipped to Charleston with ten lengths of new hose, a hundred fire helmets, a white helmet for the chief, and a supply of red shirts and trumpets. The ship sank en route. New York's smoke-eaters then duplicated the gift. Thus two years after the war, the firemen of North and South were reunited, although it took generations for this solidarity to be reflected by other persons in the community.

The Professional Manner

Cincinnati's introduction of a department of paid firemen was watched with much interest by municipal authorities, volunteer firemen, and insurance company rate makers. The efficiency of well-trained, disciplined men who were instantly available for duty became increasingly apparent. But political and social pressures resisted change in many cities for a generation or more. The desire to avoid ruffianism was perhaps the strongest single force that led to the creation of the paid fire departments. Year after year, the Annual Report of the chief engineer of the Cincinnati Fire Department contained such words as these which appeared in the 1860 presentation: "Again I must allude to the peaceful, quiet disposition of the Firemen."

One of the earliest professional departments was that of Providence, Rhode Island, where paid firemen were engaged on March 1, 1854. Unlike Cincinnati, St. Louis, and Louisville, which were other pioneers in this field, Providence did not even have a steam fire engine at that time; the city was serviced by eleven hand pumpers and one hook and ladder truck. Providence's Chief Taylor reported in May, 1855, that "the change from the volunteer to the paid system has been an important one, and it must be evident that many good results have followed from it; such as the excellent order maintained by the department at all times when on duty, the quiet in and around the engine houses, and the harmony which has prevailed."

New Orleans, always unique, had its own peculiar experience with hired firemen. The Crescent City formed its first volunteer fire company in 1829. In 1855, a professional department was estab-

Fatal Building Collapse Firemen at the 1873 Boston blaze are frantically endeavoring to rescue their comrades from the ruins of a fallen building on Essex Street. They were late.

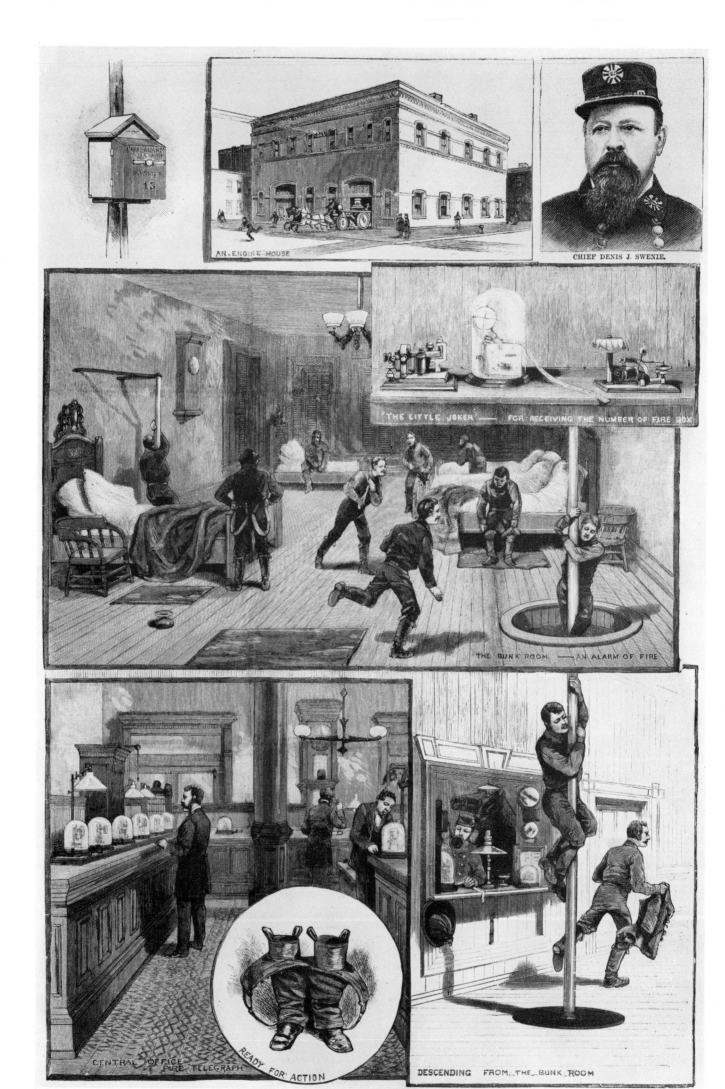

AN ENGINE HOUSE

CHIEF DENIS J. SWENIE.

"THE LITTLE JOKER" —— FOR RECEIVING THE NUMBER OF FIRE BOX

THE BUNK ROOM —— AN ALARM OF FIRE

CENTRAL OFFICE FIRE TELEGRAPH

READY FOR ACTION

DESCENDING FROM THE BUNK ROOM

lished; but this proved to be so poorly organized and so inefficient that it was disbanded in the same year. Instead, the Firemen's Charitable Association was given a contract at seventy thousand dollars per year to protect the city from fire. Fire protection was supplied by a contractor until 1890, when a conventionally organized department of paid firemen was established.

Chicago had its first professional firemen in 1858, but the department was completely made over again after the Great Fire of 1871. Other paid departments, as in Boston, were re-established after the lesson of some vast local conflagrations, usually with the advice of fire chiefs from other cities and of insurance underwriters.

New York's professional fire department was created in 1865. One of the last big cities to make the inevitable change was Philadelphia, where the spirit of Benjamin Franklin's first volunteer fire company successfully resisted the new order until 1871.

The change from amateur to professional status was not accepted with equanimity by any means. Numerous volunteer firemen were prepared to shed blood (even their own) to keep their privileged positions, and there were many reports of assaults upon the new professionals. Volunteer firemen who accepted employment in the paid departments were frequently reviled as traitors by their old comrades-at-arms. In New York, one volunteer

Alarm of Fire (opposite) A composite drawing of what happened in Chicago when someone turned in an alarm on that box in the upper left corner. Time: 1886.

The Alarm The chief thing wrong with this illustration of a New York firehouse is that the men are reaching the apparatus before the horses do. It didn't happen that way in any well-trained fire department. As soon as the locks on their stalls were tripped, the horses dashed to their places under the suspended harness.

fireman who voted to disband his company in favor of the paid department was dishonorably expelled by his fellows, even though the volunteers had been legislated out of existence. In St. Louis, some of the original professional firemen carried pistols, fearful of the vengeance of their late companions.

Although the red shirt and black leather helmet were long the symbols of the volunteer fireman, many of the first professional smoke-eaters objected to wearing uniforms when not at fires; in New York, some men refused to report for duty when they learned that they had to wear blue uniforms even when going to or from the firehouses. Such uniforms were denounced as the livery of hirelings. In an effort to combat this feeling, New York's fire commissioners (who were civilian executives and not men on combat duty) devised uniforms for themselves, which they wore conspicuously.

It was a long time before the spirit of intercompany competition disappeared in the paid fire departments, for too many of the men were ex-volunteers who had grown up in that sort of tradition. Men of different companies would meet to see whose engine could pump water to the greatest height against a Liberty pole or a church spire. One throwback to the competitive days of the

volunteers was revealed by Battalion Chief Conley of the New York Fire Department: in 1898, when he joined Engine Company No. 213, there was a great rivalry between that crew and Engine Company No. 229. By reason of a peculiarity in the electric fire alarm telegraph circuit, 213 got the alarms some seconds before 229 did, and the former company would gallop to an intersection of streets which 229 would have to pass. As soon as 229 dashed by, 213 would come up from behind and, as 213's horses had had time to catch their second wind, Conley's boys would overtake the other company, in the old tradition of "passing" and disgracing a rival en route to a fire.

The professional firemen were kept under strict discipline, and feuds involving firemen were virtually nonexistent. But even in the twentieth century, one great feud between New York's firemen and policemen broke out. At a fire in 1904, one fireman collapsed in the street from smoke inhalation. A young policeman attempted to carry the unconscious man to an ambulance; but Edward Croker, chief of the fire department, believed that the fireman would soon recover and required no medical aid. Croker ordered the policeman to let go of the senseless man and, when the order was ignored, the chief directed several of his smoke-eaters to toss the policeman into the street. The tossed policeman soon returned with some of his fellow bluecoats, and the firemen turned hose lines on these strange persons who would not heed the orders of a fire chief, whereupon the policemen drew their revolvers. Order was restored, but for years the feud only awaited an incident to rekindle itself.

Yet jealousies and rivalries were, in general, quickly curbed by officers of the professional departments, who were interested only in efficiency. Flamboyant company names were changed to more efficient if less personal numbers; men were recruited and promoted because of ability rather than influence or brawling ability; a new generation of firemen who studied their calling on a pro-

Fire From Above New York City's new elevated railway was a constant source of danger in the 1870's. A live coal carelessly dropped by a workman has fallen onto a load of cotton, with results that may be seen. Horses have been removed from the truck to a place of greater safety.

Civil Service Examinations (opposite) New York City was one of the first municipalities to have Civil Service Examinations for prospective firemen.

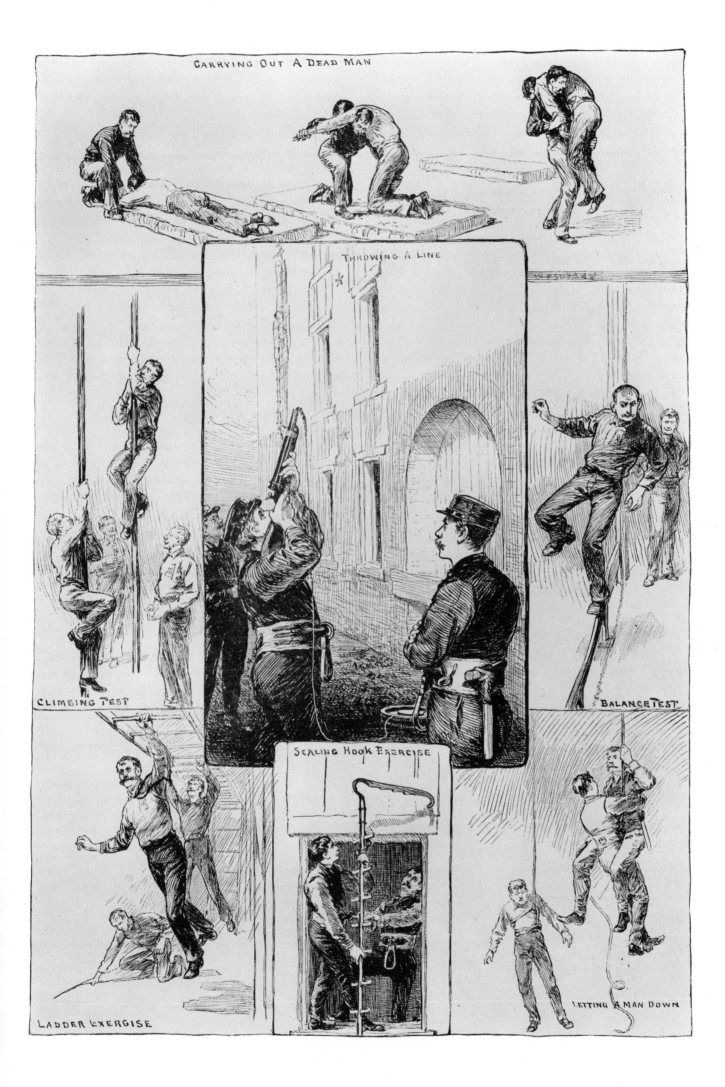

CARRYING OUT A DEAD MAN

THROWING A LINE

CLIMBING TEST

BALANCE TEST

SCALING HOOK EXERCISE

LADDER EXERCISE

LETTING A MAN DOWN

fessional basis was born. By 1870, several European cities sent their top fire officials to the United States to study the efficiency and methods of the new professionals. Today, audiences are invariably mystified when, during the second act of Gilbert and Sullivan's *Iolanthe*, one character sings:

> *Oh, Captain Shaw!*
> *Type of true love kept under!*
> *Could thy brigade*
> *With cold cascade*
> *Quench my great love, I wonder?*

But when those words were penned in 1882, Captain Eyre Massey Shaw, C.B., Chief Officer of the Metropolitan Fire Brigade of London, was well known to the professional firemen of the United States, for he had twice crossed the Atlantic to study the fire-fighting techniques of the American departments.

That the fire-fighting techniques of the United States were unusually successful was well recognized by European firemen, some of whom felt, however, that this was not attributable to any inherent natural superiority. A writer observed in 1902 that "the Germans and the French say that we ought to have the best fire-departments in the world, because we have more fires than any other country, and, consequently, more experience in fighting them."

But that was only part of the answer. Two of the greatest characteristics of Americans are organizational skill and mechanical genius, and both of these talents were devoted wholeheartedly to the professional fire departments. Equipment was constantly being improved by a variety of manufacturers; fire commissioners in the larger communities were counseled by retired army officers on discipline and by insurance company executives on efficiency. One of the first awards to be established by the paid fire department in New York was the Stephenson Medal for *efficiency*.

Civil Service provided fire department appointments in most of the larger communities long before the value of such selections was recognized in

A Battering Ram   The firemen in the foreground are using a heavy battering ram. Meanwhile, the "hooksie" men on this wintry night will try to get through an upper window. The two steamers dashing down from the background will surely be needed.

THE BURNING OF CHICAGO.

This terrible Conflagration commenced on Sunday evening, Oct. 8th, 1871, and continued until stopped by the rain on Tuesday Morning, Oct. 10th, consuming the whole of the Business portion of the City, all the Public Buildings, Hotels, Newspaper Offices and Rail Road Depots, and extending over an area of Five square Miles. It is estimated that upward of 500 lives were lost 150,000 people were rendered homeless, and property to the amount of 200,000,000 of dollars were destroyed.

The Great Chicago Fire This Currier & Ives lithograph presents a general view of the great conflagration. The force of galelike winds may be seen. *National Board of Fire Underwriters*

other fields. Many fire departments established their own training schools; in some of the big cities, fire colleges for advanced study by officers were created.

The courage and devotion to duty of the old volunteer firemen could not be improved upon by the paid smoke-eaters. But the professional manner referred to organization, supervision, equipment, practice, and "know how." Without unswerving loyalty to the "good old days," the professional departments enjoyed an atmosphere that was much more receptive to changes and improvements.

The introduction of professional fire departments did not mean that great fires no longer could rage out of hand. For reasons beyond the control of

the paid smoke-eaters, such infernos could and did occur. Such was the Great Chicago Fire.

CHICAGO S FIRE OF 1871

It may not have been cow-induced, but a fire did break out in a cowshed in the rear of Mrs. O'Leary's one-story frame building on the northeast corner of Dekoven and Jefferson streets in Chicago. It was the evening of October 8, 1871.

Any alarm caused great apprehension in the minds of Chicago's firemen at that time. There had been no heavy rain since July 3, during which time the total rainfall had been but 2½ inches. One result was that wells and cisterns had dried up. Another result was that wooden buildings and side-

Destruction in Chicago Wabash Avenue, near Harrison Street—Federal employees are frantically removing United States mail from the doomed post office building on the right. Draymen received fantastic fees for removing personal belongings.

walks were dry as tinder. And Chicago, as a rapidly growing metropolis, was a city of wooden buildings. Even factories were of wood. There were 56 miles of wood-block pavement and 651 miles of wooden sidewalks.

As a result, alarms prior to the Great Fire had been many, and the firemen were physically exhausted. Eight days of minor fires had been endured. On the night before this fire, every available smoke-eater had been working desperately at another conflagration, where an area of some sixteen acres had been swept by flames. Several fire engines had been destroyed in that sixteen-hour battle.

Mrs. O'Leary's fire began in the same section of the city, and it was hoped that the burnt-out area would check the rapid advance of the blaze. But a tornado-like wind acted as a blowpipe and drove the fire hundreds of feet at a gust. There was "a furious shower of livid coals and fire brands." Rarely had Chicago known such a violent wind. Hence burnt-out areas left by the previous night's fire did not check the advancing flames, which merely swirled across the open spaces until contact was made with wood buildings several blocks away.

"Nothing but the destruction of Pompei can outline the savageness and rapidity of [the fire's] career," wrote a visitor. "It fed on everything."

Chicago had a department of seventeen steamers to protect 334,270 persons, but the fourteen pumpers in service on October 8 were hopelessly inadequate for the task. When the municipal waterworks were consumed by the flames, steamers had to pump directly from the lake or other bodies of water. Hose was abandoned as flames drove the steamers back; several fire engines had to be left to the rapidly advancing fires.

Panic seized the city as fires constantly sprang up in new quarters. Trucks were engaged at fantastic prices to haul away any household effects or merchandise to places of safety, but the investment frequently was futile. Mobs snatched goods from heavily laden wagons, and in some instances a teamster would empty his vehicle as soon as he had been paid for loading it. And there was no one to whom to complain.

Fire engines were rushed in from other communities, but the chaos of 76,000 Chicagoans in flight impeded the entry of this help. Apparatus came from all parts of the state; a special train brought three companies from Cincinnati under the command of the venerable Miles Greenwood, the nation's first chief of a professional fire department.

When a steamer ran out of fuel, eager citizens would feed it with wood hastily snatched from a sidewalk.

Other help was becoming available, too. General Philip Sheridan used United States troops to control the mobs. The soldiers also leveled buildings on State and Wabash streets in an effort to create open spaces before the advancing flames.

Less than a month after the fire, Frederick Law Olmsted wrote that "in not more than a dozen cases have the four walls of any of the great blocks, or any of the buildings, been left standing together. It is the exception to find even a single corner or chimney holding together to a height of more than twenty feet."

The total fire loss aggregated some $200,000,000. But the citizens had at least one comforting note in their diapason of grief. According to a contemporary account, "The tax-books were consumed."

Financial aid poured in from communities all over the world. A group of Englishmen even sent over a collection of books to revitalize the Chicago Public Library. But this gift caused great embarrassment; for amidst all its growing pains, Chicago never had gotten around to providing such a library in the first place.

BOSTON'S FIRE OF 1872

On October 28, 1871, the chief of the Boston Fire Department wrote a report on his visit to the smoking ruins of Chicago. "I hope," he declared, "that our recently appointed Inspector of Buildings . . . will vehemently urge, and not only urge, but demand, that all Mansard or French roofs shall be so finished as to afford us protection from any serious conflagration from that cause." For just about a year, the specter of Mansard roofs hung over the chief. Then it happened. "For the thing which I greatly feared is come upon me, and that which I was afraid of is come unto me." (Job 3:25.) It was Mansard roofs.

November 8, 1872, was a beautiful Saturday, with only a gentle breeze. At a quarter past seven o'clock that evening, a fire broke out in a large four-story granite building at the southeast corner of Sumner and Livingston streets. An alarm was transmitted promptly from Box 52, from which more serious alarms had been sent in a twenty-five-year span than from Boston's other five hundred fire boxes combined. Yet the response of the professional firemen was anything but prompt. Virtually all of the fire horses in the city had been disabled by distemper; only six such animals were available to drag the heavy apparatus on that night.

The Great Boston Fire The destruction of a newspaper office at Franklin and Hawley streets.

The fire did not wait until engines could be hauled there by manpower. The burning structure and its neighbors had tall Mansard roofs, with large open spaces similar to vacant lofts, and the flames mushroomed from one edifice to another, thanks to this artificial draft.

The firemen had other troubles. The conflagration was in the heart of Boston's shopping district, and the narrow, winding streets made the proper deployment of equipment difficult, especially without equine pulling power. Moreover, the water supply was poor.

Buildings seemed to melt rather than to burn in the intense heat. Some of the proud city's proudest old structures fell to the flames, and the venerable Old South Church and the Old State House were barely saved. Onetime homes of Benjamin Franklin, Daniel Webster, and Edward Everett were not so fortunate. Stores, warehouses, newspaper plants were consumed along with dwellings beyond count. Flames reached the busy wharves, with heavy damage to shipping.

A reporter's flaming pen recorded how the fire reached the roof of one structure, "lapping it around and flaring redly out to the gaze of the silver moon, as a fiery Sappho, pulsed with hot, passionate blood, would glare and gloat beside the ice-cold chasteness of Diana." The reactions of other observers were more earthy, and the gin mills were jammed with citizenry.

Police and troops guarded abandoned properties as well as possible. The Commons was piled high with furniture and merchandise, often without

apparent owner. Arrests for theft were many.

Boston had twenty-one steamers, seven hook and ladder trucks, eleven independent hose companies, and three chemical wagons at that time. But personnel was woefully short. There were only 106 permanent firemen, with 363 "call men" who could be summoned—if they could be found. Neighboring communities rushed in reinforcements, and a number of ancient hand pumpers was called into service.

Within the next day and a. half, eight hundred buildings were destroyed. The property loss was probably close to $100,000,000, although some estimates reached a figure of $125,000,000. More than thirty insurance companies had to settle up their business or to reduce capital. At least twelve lives were lost.

The cause of the fire never was ascertained.

THE BROOKLYN THEATER FIRE

The best trained professional fire departments are sometimes helpless because the full force of catastrophe has struck before an alarm can be sounded. It is noteworthy that two of the most disastrous theater fires took place in communities that had outstandingly competent fire departments.

On the evening of December 5, 1876, a capacity crowd was enjoying Kate Claxton's performance in *The Two Orphans* at the Brooklyn Theater in Brooklyn, New York. At about eleven o'clock, the scenery caught fire from spotlights. A backstage worker attempted to beat out the flames with a stick, but the blaze ran along the ceiling, out of his reach. The clumsy fire-fighting efforts became audible to the actors on the stage, and H. S. Murdoch hesitated. "Go on," said Miss Claxton, "they will put it out; there will be a panic—go on." Murdoch continued his lines; but people in the first few rows, smelling smoke, began to get up. "We are between you and the flames," Miss Claxton called reassuringly. But as the symptoms of fire became more menacing, one actor stepped forward and declared: "Ladies and gentlemen, there will be no more of the play, of course; you can all go out if you will only keep quiet."

At that moment some smoke drifted over the footlights, and a man screamed, "It's time to get out of here!" Instantly everyone was on his feet, and the panic was on. The center aisle was imme-

Reinforcements for Boston To help out the desperate Boston firemen, apparatus and men were rushed from other communities. Equipment of the Worcester Fire Department is being unloaded at the Boston depot.

The Brooklyn Theatre Fire The actors are doing their best to prevent a panic, but an asbestos curtain (now required by law) would have been much more effective in containing the blaze.

The Temple Theatre Fire On December 27, 1886, this Philadelphia theatre burned down amidst spectacular fire fighting. The building already is well laddered at an early stage of the blaze.

diately blocked hopelessly. Senseless fights began everywhere. A draft caused by numerous opening doors drove the fire to the canvas dome of the theater, and the smoke was sufficient to choke innumerable persons.

Most of the people sitting in the orchestra were able to escape; but the winding passages in the balconies made escape extremely difficult. Throughout the theater, people became lost in the ever-thickening smoke. "Don't follow me," cried an actor when he noticed theater-goers running after him; "I may be leading you to your death!"

Numerous fatalities were directly attributed to a door at the foot of the balcony steps that had been locked. The loss was estimated to have been between 250 and 290 persons; identification of even the *number* of persons killed by the flames was impossible. One hundred unidentifiable dead were buried together in city-leased ground in Greenwood Cemetery.

The managers of all other Brooklyn theaters suspended business for the balance of the week. The Brooklyn Theater Fire Relief Association raised $47,455.47 for the victims. The site of the theater later was occupied by the Brooklyn *Eagle,* until that newspaper went out of existence in 1955.

THE IROQUOIS THEATER FIRE

If there is a heavy loss of life in a theater fire, the catastrophe usually is caused by reason of the building's being too ancient and too old-fashioned. But at one of the worst of such fires, the heavy loss of life was attributable to the fact that the building was too new. Safety devices were not yet in operation.

When the Iroquois Theater in Chicago first opened its doors to an expectant crowd on November 23, 1903, the structure was billed as "the most perfect theatre in America." Five weeks later, it was a horrible shambles.

The luxurious building was located in the most prominent business district in Chicago, bordering on Randolph and Dearborn streets. Luxury extended to the boxes, the back walls of which were covered with heavy plush. Even the exit openings were draped with plush. The wooden seats throughout the theater were stuffed with hemp.

On Wednesday, December 30, an afternoon performance was being given. At three-thirty, a floodlight caught fire; the light had been set up on a scaffold directly over the switchboard on the stage. Many persons saw the flare-up, and a private fireman tried to extinguish the small fire with an extinguisher. But the overheated light set fire to some scenery. There were standpipe arrangements on the stage, although hose had not been supplied as yet in this new building. And there was as yet no water in the pipes. In the files was a complaint about this very situation which a fire captain in the district had submitted.

While someone rushed to the nearest fire alarm box (which was several hundred feet away), an actor, Eddie Foy, stepped calmly up to the footlights. He reminded the audience of the safe construction of the building, and he asked everybody to remain calm. Then the curtain was lowered. But the other actors rushed to safety through the stage exits, and the draft from these opening doors caused the curtain to swell out against the proscenium wall, where the curtain became entangled about twenty feet above the stage.

Two huge ventilators above the stage probably could have allowed the flames to escape upward, but the ventilators were not yet in operation. Thus flames and hot air, with no other escape possible, were forced out into the auditorium through the gap in the dangling curtain. A sheet of flame leaped over the orchestra into the balcony and gallery.

Immediately there was a stampede in the darkened house, where all the lights had been extinguished to make the moonlight scene on the stage more effective. Many exit doors could not be opened. An emergency stairway from the third floor could not be used, for the ushers dutifully observed a house rule that the door should be opened only at the end of an act.

There were three stairs in front of many of the exits, and the maddened crowds stumbled on the steps. Firemen could not force their way through some of the doors, as bodies were piled six feet high within the theater.

No one in the orchestra was killed, except by persons who had jumped from the balconies or in the subsequent stampede. But the loss of life in the galleries was tremendous; it would have been more had not some painters in a building on the other side of a twelve-foot alley thrust ladders across to the theater balcony. In forty minutes, the entire stage was destroyed, as well as portions of the auditorium. The death toll exceeded six hundred lives.

Iroquois Theatre   (opposite) These scenes of the terrible Chicago theatre disaster appeared in a supplement to *Harper's Weekly* that appeared on January 9, 1904.

View from the Stage, toward the Right of the wrecked Auditorium

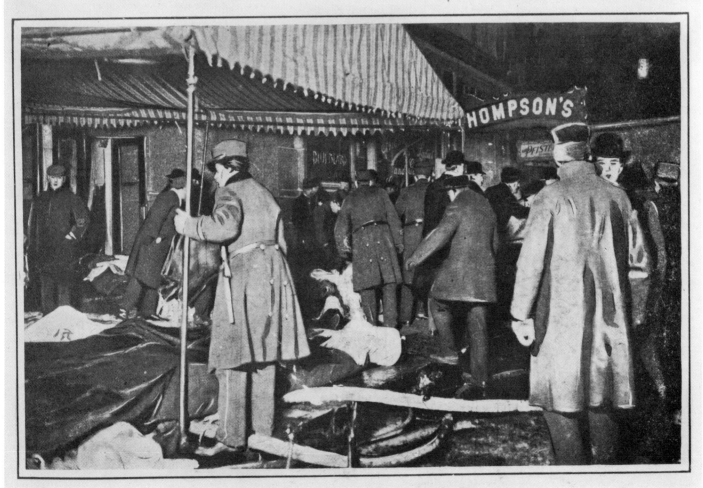

Scene in Front of the Theatre during the Fire

Firemen's Contest Hose-laying competition at Jamaica, New York, in 1885. Except for the trumpets and the style of the hose cart, this might have been depicted today.

The Volunteers Hold Fast

The establishment of paid fire departments did not completely sound the knell of the volunteers by any means. In the larger communities, professional firemen became standard municipal equipment. But in other places, unpaid smoke-eaters continued to serve. A publication of the Home Insurance Company estimated that there are a quarter of a million volunteer firemen in the United States today.

Without the active help of the volunteers, the paid departments could not have proven themselves. Not only did the unpaid groups furnish recruits; they also supplied guidance and occasionally equipment. Thus when St. Louis established a professional fire department comprised entirely of engine companies, Lafayette Hook & Ladder Company No. 1 remained in existence to lend its truck and its services when necessary. How these volunteers actually felt about the professional system is indicated by the company motto: "Public servants, not hirelings."

The chief engineer of the paid fire department in Baltimore expressed his feelings in his annual report for 1863: "I cannot, however, pass without acknowledging many kind favors from the old members of the volunteer organizations. . . . Voluntary associations are all liable to abuse and yet none, throughout the width and breadth of the land, had less errors, if so they may be called, as that [sic] of our volunteer fire departments."

A contemporary newspaper pointed out a vacuum that would be left by the passing of the unpaid smoke-eaters: "What now shall we have in the city to supply the annual balls given by the various companies so numerously that they occupy nearly every dancing night of the winter? What will take the place of the jovial surprise parties continually occurring during the winter at the fire-houses, where the sisters and sweethearts and wives of the laddies enjoyed themselves so genially and hospitably, as there was no other opportunity in all other social assemblies of our working classes, and which were to our most aristocratic, richest, and best educated young men an absolute relief from the stately balls and stiff-backed parties of the upper ten? What will become of the excursions, the clam-bakes, the country jaunts, with music and dancing, that the fun-loving firemen indulged in all summer long? Maybe there were rough fellows among the fire boys; but they were generous and honest, anyhow, they claimed; and though they had once and awhile a little fight among each other, they were always orderly as a body, they always subserved the good of the city, they were the pride of all great parades."

If the professional firemen at times regarded parades as too frivolous for their professional prestige (or just as an unmitigated nuisance), the volunteers did not. It was noted in St. Louis in 1880: "As in the case of the tea parties, the lady friends of the members took the greatest interest in these affairs, and dainty, dexterous fingers were busily employed for weeks before the auspicious day in forming decorations for the engines, reels, &c."

Colorado Collegians This picture, taken in the early 1890's, shows a volunteer company composed of men from Colorado College. The hose cart, furnished by the town of Colorado Springs, was loaded with nine hundred feet of hose, as hydrants were very widely spaced at that time. The house was located on the north side of Cache La Poudre Street between Nevada and Tejon streets. The company was replaced by a paid department. *Dr. Lester Williams*

Not infrequently, professional and volunteer firemen served side by side. Thus Danbury, Connecticut, changed from a volunteer to a partly paid department on September 18, 1889, with an organization having two branches: four companies on a paid basis and seven on an unpaid basis.

Where the volunteers were supplanted by professionals, the former lingered on long after their services, equipment, and advice were useless. Exempt firemen's associations and similar groups existed as long as the old volunteers lived—and sometimes longer. But the spiritual if not the physical descendants of the volunteer firemen live on today in another form: the buffs. The word "buff" apparently refers to the buff coats or buff facings on uniforms worn at parades by the old volunteers, as distinguished from the blue uniforms that were worn from the start by the professionals. Thus a buff referred originally to one who had been a volunteer fireman before the professional era. Today a buff is a person who is passionately interested in the activities (and sometimes in the welfare) of firemen. The ordinary buff is apt to be considered by laymen to be a hanger-on at a firehouse; but he is far more than that. He has a tremendous knowledge of the whole background of fire fighting; he knows equipment; he is familiar with locations of companies and of fireboxes; he has more than a smattering of knowledge of the technical side of the fireman's trade. He helps out the firemen, whether it be in the fetching of coffee or in the obtaining of merchandise at wholesale prices. In short, he loves fire fighting and fire equipment, and he will leave his home or office at almost any hour of the day or night to chase a "worker" (a fire where "all hands" actually are at work).

In many communities, there are regular organizations of buffs or, as they are sometimes called, "sparks." Among these may be mentioned the Box 4 Associates of Worcester, Massachusetts; the Box Seven Association of Dayton, Ohio; the Box 8 Club of St. Louis, Missouri; the Box 12 Associates of Detroit, Michigan; the Box 13 Associates of Cincinnati, Ohio; the Box 14 Association of Jackson, Michigan; the Box 15 Club of Columbus, Ohio; the Box 15 Club of Los Angeles, California; the Box 17 Club of Albany, New York; the Box 21 Associates of Dayton, Ohio; the Box 22 Club of New Haven, Connecticut; the Box 23 Associates of Lansing, Michigan; the Box 27 Associates of Springfield, Ohio; the Box 35 Associates of Minneapolis, Minnesota; the Box 42 Associates of Detroit, Michigan; the Box 44 Association of Woburn, Massachusetts; the Box 52 Association of Boston, Massachusetts; the Box 54 Club of Teaneck, New Jersey; the Box 65 Club of Bay City, Michigan; the Box 113 Club of Pontiac, Michigan; the Box 212 Associates of Lexington, Kentucky; the 255 Club of Brooklyn, New York; the 321 Association of Grand Rapids, Michigan; the Box 414 Association of Baltimore, Maryland; the 476 Club of Philadelphia, Pennsylvania; the 5-11 Club of Chicago, Illinois; the Box 1776 Association of Philadelphia, Pennsylvania; the Box Alarm Association of Sacramento, California; the Bell and Siren Club of Newark, New Jersey; the Boston Sparks Association; the Brockton Reserve Firefighters of Brockton, Massachusetts; the Burlington Third Alarmers of Burlington, Iowa; the Chicago Fire Fans Association; the Detroit Fire Buffs Association; the Extra Alarm Fire Association

Champions Every proud community doubtless thought that its own fire chasers were the fastest volunteer fire company in the whole United States, but in Whitestone, New York, this was no idle boast. This picture shows Columbia Hose Company, which won the national championship race with a hose reel at the National Firemen's Association in St. Louis in 1904. *Captain Clarence Meek*

of Cincinnati, Ohio; the Fire Alarm Club of Cleveland, Ohio; the Fire Bell Club of Milwaukee, Wisconsin; the Fire Bell Club of New York, New York; the Fire Siren Club of Chicago, Illinois; the Gong Club of Jersey City, New Jersey; the Hoop and Hammer Club of Hillside, New Jersey; the Milwaukee Third Alarm Association; the Nashville Fire Buffs Club of Nashville, Tennessee; the Phoenix Society of San Francisco, California; the Second Alarmers Association of Davenport, Iowa; the Second Alarmers Association of Philadelphia, Pennsylvania; the Signal 7-7 Fire Club of Brooklyn, New York; the Signal 22 Association of Trenton, New Jersey; the Smoke Eaters Club of Norfolk, Virginia; the Tapper Club of Boston, Massachusetts; the Third Alarm Association of New York, New York; the Third Alarm Club of Saginaw, Michigan; the Three Alarm Club of Bayonne, New Jersey. The parent organization of a number of

these groups is International Fire Buff Associates, Inc.

Where the volunteers were not supplanted by professionals, these unpaid men continued to risk life, limb, and job for the service of the community (or for the adventure of it all, or for both). Today's volunteers are not the rowdies that their forefathers so often were; there is more respect for law and authority generally, and police departments usually are equipped to deal with hooliganism now. Volunteer fire departments are no longer "curious outlets for pioneer exuberance that combined firefighting with quarreling among themselves," as was said about the Pittsburgh fire companies of 1845. But otherwise the volunteer of today performs the same functions that his red-shirted ancestors did. Today's volunteers must have a technical knowledge and skill that was not expected of his predecessors, who lived in a simpler, nontechnical age.

Ready! Neptune Hose Company No. 2 of Galena, Illinois, is ready for a parade, a contest with another company, or even a fire. Time: about 1889. *Illinois State Historical Library*

An Ohio Veterans' Company The Philadelphia-style hand pumper has an ornate decorated panel of a traditional fireman-saves-damsel type, which originally was a Currier lithograph. *Western Reserve Historical Society*

The professional fire departments brought an efficiency and technical perfection to their trade that had been unknown in the strictly volunteer days. But the more alert volunteer fire departments quickly learned the new techniques. Sometimes a professional smoke-eater would be hired to teach the local boys the *science* of fire fighting; other volunteers learned from observation, reading, and experience. At precisely the time when the paid firemen were justifying their engagement, the amateurs were impressing the remainder of the world with their own performance. International exhibits of fire-fighting techniques began in Paris in 1867, and American companies from that year on could be counted upon to win far more than their share of the prizes. At the International Fire Congress in Paris in 1900, for example, the Kansas City Fire

Department team of fourteen men won over eight thousand contestants from twenty nations. These American amateurs won a silver trophy fifteen inches high, as well as eight hundred francs, for throwing a 1¼-inch stream 180 feet vertically and 310 feet horizontally.

Without the frequent fire alarms to which their professional brethren responded, ambitious volunteers resorted to competitive drills and matches. County fairs, agricultural expositions, and single-purpose firemen's tournaments provided (and still provide) the opportunity of comparing the skill and speed of one company with another. Crack teams of volunteer firemen won recognition among persons who understand such things comparable with the laurels bestowed upon the original heroes of the Olympic games.

Cataract   (above) This is the gallant pumper crew of Cadott, Wisconsin, in about 1887. The bold title of "Cataract" appears on the apparatus, but this suggests Whittier's comment upon another engine: "The engine wet all around but kindly spared the fire." *State Historical Society of Wisconsin*

Soldiers Test a Hand Pumper   (below) This machine is being tested at Willets Point, New York. The theory of this particular drill seems to have been: since no hose line is connected to the engine, why overexert? *National Archives*

Steamer and Two-Wheeler This steamer and hose cart were used by the Hampton, Virginia, Fire Department in the early 1900's. *Hampton, Virginia, Fire Department*

When the professional fire departments first were organized, usually they purchased the largest steamer or other equipment that was available. Many volunteer companies had neither the inclination nor the funds to follow suit. An 1873 book thus referred to the smaller communities: "The popular steam fire-engine for such purposes would be about as useful as an elephant for weeding carrots!" But in time the volunteers got around to acquiring secondhand equipment well broken in by big-city use. Then the amateur smoke-eaters learned the advantage of getting their own equipment in new condition, tailored to individual requirements (or peculiarities). Today many volunteer companies have apparatus that would shame most professional departments. Special paint jobs and other features of some such equipment are inferior to none in the land.

Women have entered the armed forces but not the professional fire departments. That condition is generally true in volunteer ranks, although many generations ago the Galena, Illinois, Fire Department had a special Women's Broom Brigade.

As in the heyday of the volunteers, just anyone cannot join a volunteer fire company today. There are tests to be met with respect to physique, intelligence, availability, personality, and other matters. As in the past, some fire companies are more difficult to join than are the most exclusive social clubs. But other companies will gladly accept anyone.

Most volunteer companies today are eligible for the praise bestowed upon the system some seventy years ago: "There was no electricity in those days, but the men ran as if they had it in their boots. They were quick, hard-working fellows, without discount."

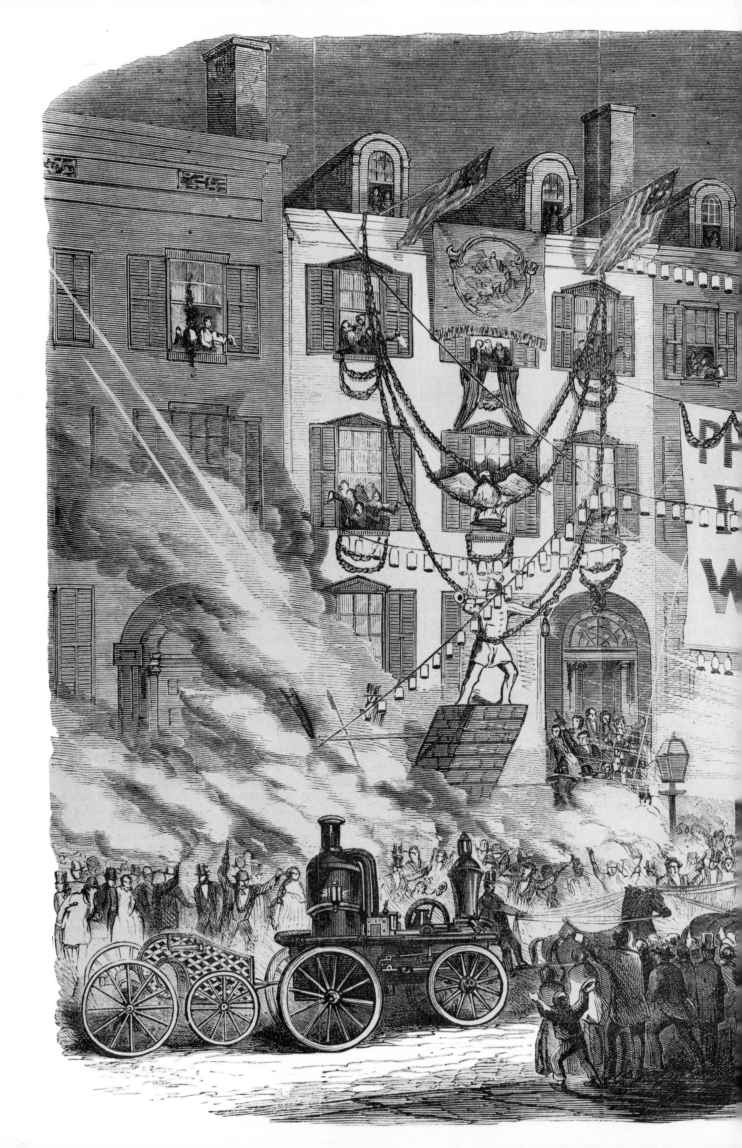

Parades

Parades were very important to the volunteer firemen. It gave the men an opportunity of identifying themselves with a pet company. It served to show the important role that firemen served in the community. It presented an excuse for dressing up the engine (or the firemen).

In a less sophisticated day, no event was complete without the appearance of the local or visiting firemen. Thus when General Lafayette paid a return visit to the United States in 1824, one of the most popular forms of diversion supplied for him was the firemen's parade; and as a result of the marquis's unflagging interest at many such parades, numerous companies changed their old names to Lafayette Hose Company, Lafayette Engine Company, etc.

Great events such as the opening of the Erie Canal or of a new reservoir, the anniversary of events such as the withdrawal of the British army in 1783, or celebrations such as military victories were the occasions for parades. And dearly did the firemen love the marches, despite the laborious work of preparation.

Some companies had their apparatus especially painted or decorated for a particular parade. Other companies adorned their equipment with bunting, flowers, or even live animals. New York's Eagle Hook & Ladder Company No. 4 sometimes attached a real eagle to its truck, while Americus Engine Company No. 6, not to be outdone, chained a tiger to the engine that already had a tiger's head painted upon it.

Visiting Firemen During a parade in New York City eight horses pull this engine past the home of the distinguished chief engineer of the New York Fire Department, Harry Howard. Howard was one of the greatest heroes in the annals of the fire department. During the Great Fire of 1835, the thirteen-year-old lad served as a runner. He went through the ranks and became chief engineer on February 3, 1857. At the age of eighty-four, he headed the firemen's division in the Bartholdi Parade, and he marched "steadily" on the slippery streets.

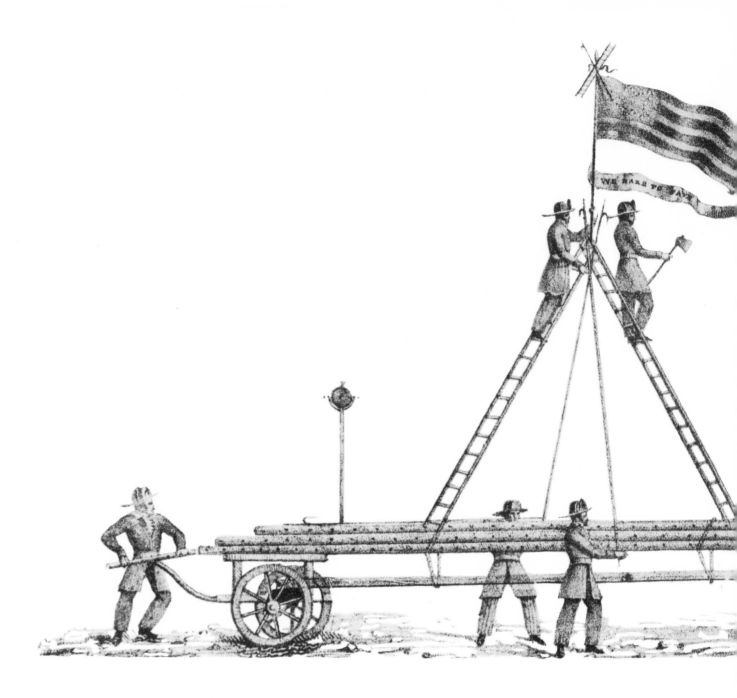

Chief engineers or foremen had special silver speaking trumpets for parades, and the toughest smoke-eater had no qualms about marching with his trumpet overflowing with flowers. Some companies had special parade or marching costumes. In Philadelphia, firemen had parade costumes of glazed hats, drab fire coats and trousers, and oilcloth capes falling over the shoulders.

Visiting celebrities sometimes were waited upon by parades of firemen. One of the most famous of these parades was occasioned by Jenny Lind's first concert in the United States in 1850. She turned over her first New York box-office receipts to local charities, including the Firemen's Widows and Orphans Fund. This was the main benevolence of "a body of men whose services she highly appreciates." The grateful firemen replied with gifts of a golden box and a copy of Audubon's *Birds of America*. This presentation was made the occasion of a procession, complete with bands and torches, and virtually the entire fire department turned out on that beautiful October night. The committee told Miss Lind in the simple language of the smoke-eater that "when her voice should cease to charm the ear, her memory would be affectionately cherished, not only in their own hearts but in the heart of every widow and orphan, whose prayers for her welfare already ascend in grateful invocation to heaven." The great coloratura was equal to the speech, and a lifetime mutual admiration society was started. "I have always regarded with admiration," she declared, "the brave and useful body of men to which you belong—The Firemen of America."

Whether firemen could participate in political parades was always a touchy question; a few com-

Hook and Ladder on Parade A pyramid of ladders and a pair of signal torches dressed up this truck for an Erie Canal Parade in 1825. The horses were for exhibition purposes only; this truck ordinarily was man-propelled

munities actually disbanded companies that showed such favoritism. But one very influential political group patterned its marching attire after firemen's costumes. In 1860, the Hartford, Connecticut, "Wide-Awakes" were formed by the Young Republican Club. A marching auxiliary was formed for political parades, the marchers wearing oilcloth firemen's hats and coats. It was understood that the movement had been supported by Hartford's fire insurance companies, for whom the costumes were an effective advertisement.

When the Prince of Wales visited New York in 1860, the firemen gave a tremendous torchlight procession in his honor on the night of October 13. There were six thousand smoke-eaters in line, and Prince Edward reviewed the marchers from the balcony of the Fifth Avenue Hotel. This was considered to have been one of the city's finest displays. James Gordon Bennett, the publisher, later declared that the prince saw at this time the possibilities of escaping from his rather strict retinue by means of a fire ladder; and with Bennett's aid, a surreptitious descent by ladder subsequently was made by the prince at eleven-thirty one evening. At eight-thirty the following morning, the prince jubilantly returned to his hotel, to be met with consternation by his staff, who thought that he had been sleeping all the while.

The English magazine *All the Year 'Round* thus portrayed a firemen's parade in 1861: "Here they come, four abreast. 'Fours,' with no very severe military air of still order and mathematical regularity, but with light, gay, swinging step, jaunty, careless, rather defiant freemen, a little self-conscious of display, but braving it out in a manly game-cock way. . . . They wear a short of shako

In Honor of the Prince of Wales

Parades for visiting firemen were a common-place, but the procession for the Prince of Wales (later Edward VII) when he visited New York on October 13, 1860, was unusually spectacular. The prince may be seen watching from a balcony as the parade passed the Fifth Avenue Hotel. Nearly five thousand men with torches were in the line of march. (Later Edward arranged for firemen to come with a thirty-five-foot ladder to his hotel, and he climbed out while his retinue slept. At 8:30 the following morning, the prince returned to his hotel and to his amazed escort party.)

PHŒNIX STEAM FIRE ENGINE Nº 3 OF DETROIT,
AS IT APPEARED IN THE FUNERAL PROCESSION OF THE LATE PRESIDENT LINCOLN, APRIL, 25TH 1865.

LITH. SAGE SONS & CO. BUFFALO, N.Y.

covered with oilskin, red flannel shirts, with black silk handkerchiefs, blowing gaily (as to the ends), tied around their throats in jaunty sailors' knots; they are all young men, some quite boys. It is evidently the manner with them to affect recklessness, so as not to appear to be drilled or drummed around to the detriment of their brave democratic freedom uniform. . . .

"These street processions are incessant in New York, and contribute much to the gayness of the street. Whether firemen, or volunteers, or political torchbearers, they are very arbitrary in their march.

They allow no omnibus, or van, or barouche, to break their ranks; and I have often seen all the immense traffic of Broadway (a street that is a mixture of Cheapside and Regent-street) stand still, benumbed, while a band of men, enclosed in a square of rope, dragged by a shining brass gun or a bran new gleaming fire-engine."

The mustering out of the volunteers did not mean an end to parades. For many years, any parade worth its salt had contingents of both professional firemen and the old volunteers. The latter apparently did not realize how this side-by-side comparison made the onlookers conscious of the far greater efficiency of the paid departments. A witness of such a parade in 1883 referred to the volunteer contingents and their old apparatus, "which made a miserable contrast with the splendid steam engines and efficiently fitted hook and ladder machines displayed by the present Department." Some spectators, seeing the seedy and inefficient equipment of the "vamps," wondered why the paid departments had been put off for so long.

The New York *Herald* thus described one parade in 1886: "Areas of flaming shirts, lines of heavy, crimson lined overcoats, squares of heavy yellow overcoats, garments of gray and blue and black! How gayly they swept by to the refrain of the band and the plaudits of the multitude! To the latter the scene was a revival of the memories of

long ago. It was the old Volunteers, with their beloved 'machine,' that were passing, with heads now grizzled, faces wrinkled, but not a whit less brave, less manly or less gritty than when they fought the flames with their primitive apparatus and fought the faction fights of long ago. . . .

"When fifty of the boys in red shirts, black trousers turned up above the mud, and big fire hats came trudging along, hauling an antiquated fire engine, the crowd cheered wildly, and the fire laddies took up the cry of 'Hi, hi, hi!' as they passed the President. The leaders of the line waved their big speaking trumpets, and the whole scene for the time was one of unrestrained joy on the part of the firemen and the crowd."

On occasions when every fireman in town was on parade, special precautions sometimes were

A Funeral Procession (opposite) Phoenix Steam Fire Engine Company No. 3, located on Clifford Street at the head of Griswold in Detroit, Michigan, participated in memorial services for President Lincoln on April 25, 1865. Note the fire department symbols that were used as ornaments on various parts of the firehouse. *Detroit Historical Museum*

Volunteer Firemen's Parade (below) This painting by Pierson and Poincy shows a parade at Canal and Royal streets in New Orleans in 1872. Note the horse-drawn steamer to the right of center. In the right foreground, a vendor appears to be selling a Creole praline to two smoke-eaters. The faces were actual portraits.

Parades Were Not Only for Volunteers
An early parade of the New York Fire Department, shortly after the men went on a professional basis.

taken: extra hose was coiled just inside the doors of the vacant firehouses, for use by policemen or civilians in case of need. Of course, in case of real need, the smoke-eaters could dash to the fire in their parade clothes.

Not all of the parades were joyous occasions. Firemen frequently paraded in funeral processions. When Andrew Jackson, the beloved "man of the people," died in 1845, the New York firemen marched in black costumes, with banners and speaking trumpets draped in black. Most of the communities through which President Lincoln's funeral train passed had mourning parades, with firemen and apparatus draped in black. In 1955, the New York Fire Department revived the old custom of having a fire engine bear in a procession the coffin of any officer who dies in service.

Baltimore Parade A parade on West Baltimore Street in about 1905. In some parades, the firemen added to the reality of it all by having a good fire under the steamer's boiler. *Peale Museum, Baltimore*

134

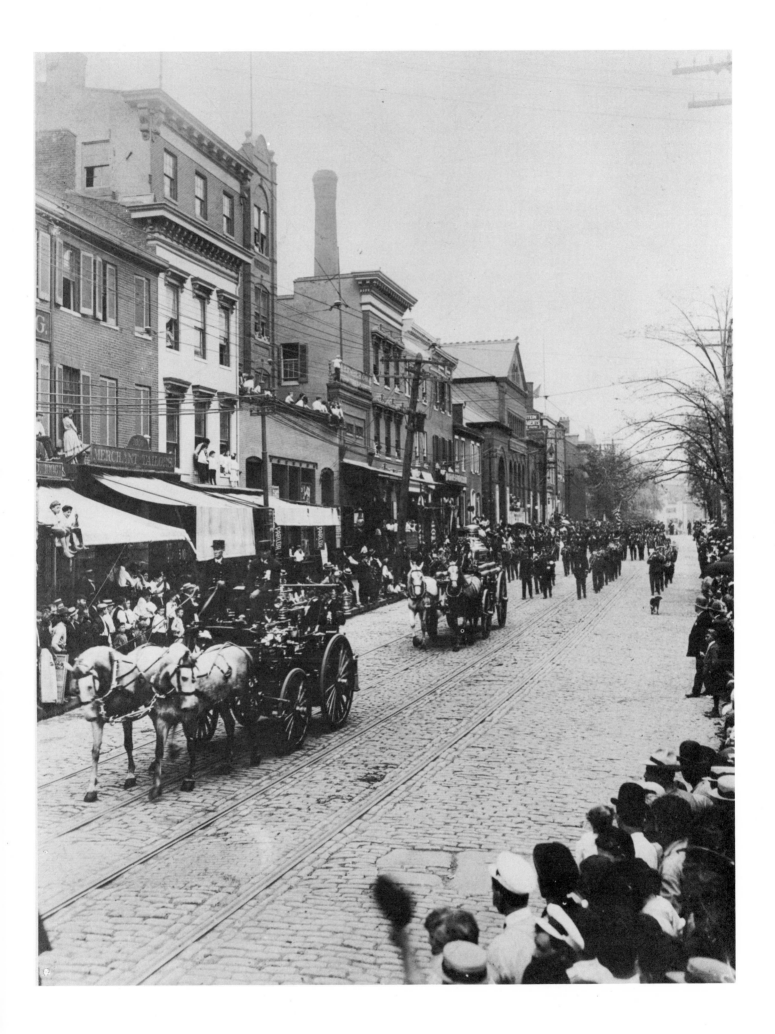

135

THE WATCHMAN.

NINE O'CLOCK BELL.

THE TOWER.

A FIRE.

MEAT MARKET

Fire Watcher   These drawings of the watch tower at Spring and Varick streets, New York, were
136   made by the celebrated artist Winslow Homer. The watchman discovered fires
                    through his trusty telescope, and he gave the alarm by strokes on a huge bell.

Inventions, Improvements and Ingenuity

COMMUNICATIONS

Prompt notification to the smoke-eaters is ever a crying need of fire fighting. For example, the Great New Orleans Fire of March 21, 1788, got out of hand because, when a drapery was ignited by a candle, the priests refused to let the church bells be sounded, as it was Good Friday. Some 856 buildings were lost as a result of tardy summoning of the firemen, and the damage sustained was neatly calculated at $2,595,561.

Until the second half of the nineteenth century, church bells were a general means of announcing the outbreak of fire. Townspeople were expected to know when the bells *should* be tolled; if they were sounded at other times, it meant fire. Furthermore, the excited clanging of church bells could betoken that this was no mere reminder that divine services were to be held. Even in communities that had regular fire bells, church sextons were supposed to broaden the coverage of the alarm by chiming in. An irritated observer thus reported on the bell system in New York in 1837: "The first in the field, the most vigorous in action, is the bell of the Middle Dutch Church. Who the ringer of that bell is, we know not; but this we will aver, that he labors with a zeal and perseverance that are quite astounding. We fancy he, now and then, gets up in his sleep to exercise his vocation."

In *Cries Of New York*, published in 1816, Samuel Wood spoke of one of the most horrible: the alarm of fire. "This is a dismal and alarming cry indeed in the night. It is generally echoed first by the watchmen, one of whom stands every night in the cupola of the city hall, to have an eye over the city, and another at the door of the jail; and immediately on the sight or cry of fire, the bells at these places ring; the alarm soon spreads, and becomes general—the bells ringing, with the cry of fire! fire! fire! from every quarter; the rattling of the engines; the burning and falling of houses; the great destruction of goods and sometimes lives."

Edgar Allan Poe brought out the horror of night summons in his poem, "The Bells":

> Hear the loud alarum bells—
> Brazen bells! . . .
> In a clamorous appealing to the mercy of
> the fire,
> In a mad expostulation with the deaf and
> frantic fire.

New York's Great Fire of 1845 was an example of how a delayed communication of alarm can cause havoc. Early on the morning of July 19, the watchman in the bell tower at City Hall apparently dozed off. The great brazen bell was not sounded when a fire broke out in a sperm oil establishment at three o'clock. When the firemen ultimately were summoned, the flames had spread to several other structures. But even then the blaze doubtless could have been confined, except for the fact that one of the ignited buildings was a warehouse where saltpeter was stored. The resultant explosion shattered "a million panes of glass." This explosion shook the city "like an earthquake." The heavy gates of several banks were burst open by the force of the blast. Thirty persons were killed and hundreds were injured. Before the flames were subdued, three hundred buildings had been de-

An Early Fire Alarm Telegraph   Well ahead of its time was the telegraph system used by the
Boston Fire Department. This scene depicts headquarters in 1852.

stroyed with a property loss of seven million dollars. One of the losses was a much-used old fire alarm bell, which was destroyed when its tower crashed. "But this disastrous fire silenced forever the brazen tongue that had for a century given forth its warning notes. Its only enemy at last prevailed, and one decisive victory compensated the fire fiend for many a defeat of yore."

In 1851, the telegraphic fire alarm was invented in Boston. The transmission of fire alarms by telegraph directly to each house was hailed as a remarkably forward step, and, thirty years later, it was recalled that "although the old-fashioned engines were then in use, it was said to be hardly possible for a great fire to occur again."

But the speed of electricity was not instantly available even after fireboxes were installed. In the beginning, the fireboxes were kept locked. Thus when a fire was discovered, a passer-by had to hunt frantically for a policeman, fireman, or other privileged person who carried a key. In time, "respectable" citizens were allowed to carry keys. Then someone realized that boxes could be provided without a lock.

HOSE

The principle of fire fighting has not changed radically since the days of Prometheus, who allegedly stole the fire of the gods. But the means of getting water or some other blanketing force on a fire are subject to constant change.

Until the close of the eighteenth century, fire engines could only pump water directly into the blaze. If the fire was beyond the reach of the nozzle mounted atop the pumper, nothing could be done except with buckets. The invention of hose was a tremendous step forward. Firemen could enter the burning structure with a hose line and go directly up to the flames, while the engine was operated on the street some floors below. Also, the engine did not have to be supplied with water by buckets; by means of suction, an engine could draw water through a hose line directly from a cistern or lake. The first hose was made of leather, which was riveted in sections.

In 1803, the Philadelphia Hose Company was established as the world's first fire company of that type. These men did not have a pumper; they merely carried six hundred feet of leather hose that could be used to service other crews at a fire. In 1825, the mayor of Boston declared that "every hundred feet of hose is as effectual as the presence of sixty men with buckets."

OTHER "EXTINGUISHERS"

By the dawn of the nineteenth century, fireboats were used in localities which had shipping to protect. In 1800, New York City provided its smoke-eaters with a whale boat decked over with planking. A regular hand pumper was permanently set into the deck. For propulsion of the craft, long oars or sweeps were provided. In the ordinary process of evolution, fireboats used the same power plant to move the craft and to operate the pumps: human muscle, steam, electricity, gasoline, or Diesel engines.

Chemicals were long used for the quenching of fires; but when electricity began to be used in factories and homes, there was a special need for chemical extinguishers, as water is a conductor.

Likewise, portable extinguishers can be brought to inaccessible places and may be placed in service before a hose line can be stretched. The development of industrial fire hazards spurred the search for new chemical extinguishers. Thus the invention of the airplane brought about the need for a fast-acting chemical that could be used on electricity and gasoline without the delay of hydrant connections.

THE HOOK AND LADDER TRUCK

One of the manifestations of civilization is progressively higher buildings. To the firemen, several problems are thus presented and compounded. It is necessary to rescue persons who are too high up to jump safely. It is imperative that water or other extinguishing materials be brought to places that cannot be reached from the street. And a tall building, for certain obvious mathematical reasons, contains more burnable materials than does a smaller one.

Unsnarling the Hose Lines One of the curses of a fire is the manner in which traffic is tied up by hose lines. Here is a device that was tried in 1894 to raise the lines above vehicular traffic, such as streetcars. Even today, this problem has not been solved; in fact, solution is rarely attempted.

Soda and Acid (above) An 1874 experiment with the use of chemicals as fire-fighting agents. Soda is a very common type of fire extinguisher today. But there is also carbontetrachloride, carbon dioxide, and a variety of others.

Chicago Chemical Company (opposite) The Chicago Fire Department acquired this Babcock chemical fire extinguisher in 1872, shortly after the Big Fire. The well-bearded firemen must have faced many occupational hazards. *Chicago Historical Society*

In the American colonies, ladders originally were not considered to be in the category of portable fire equipment. In 1659, Boston ordered six ladders for public use, and this apparatus was kept in places where need might be anticipated. New York adopted the same method: thus Hook & Ladder Company No. 2 kept its ladders hung up in City Hall Park, so that the first passing persons (firemen or otherwise) could carry this equipment to the scene of the fire. Fellowship Fire Company of Philadelphia stored ladders in various strategic places throughout the city.

Late in the eighteenth century, two- and four-wheeled trucks were used to transport ladders. These vehicles, when loaded, weighed far more than did the pumpers of that day; and it was usually necessary to have iron projections from the truck for runners to grasp, in addition to the wagon tongue or the rope that was attached to the front of the wagon. But as trucks grew longer, or as traffic made maneuvering more difficult, the problem

of getting the rear part of the vehicle around corners became acute. Shortly before 1850, there was devised an independent steering device for the rear wheels, the tiller. Sometimes this could be manipulated from street level; in time, the tillerman sat atop the truck and steered the back wheels from there.

Until well past the mid-point of the nineteenth century, ladders were sufficiently short so that they could be carried about freely by firemen or by unschooled pedestrians. If the ladders were too short to reach a trapped person at a fire, several ladders could be spliced together with ropes; in the coastal cities, at least, there were always enough sailors around who understood the science of knots. That some impatient persons jumped rather than awaited the fastening together of ladders by excited amateurs is understandable.

In 1861, an extension ladder was demonstrated in New York: two ladders were permanently fastened together in parallel formation, so that one

Extension Ladder Demonstration

(opposite page) New York had its first exhibition of an extension ladder in 1861, when Lafayette Hook & Ladder Company No. 6 gave a demonstration in City Hall Park. The same location was the scene of this 1873 demonstration of an aerial ladder. Note the men in a bucket near the top of the ladder. At the extreme right are weights to balance the men on the rungs. Two years later, during a demonstration of a ninety-seven-foot aerial ladder in eight sections, the wood snapped, and a battalion chief and two other men on the ladder were hurled to their deaths.

Risks of a Ladderman

(right) Fires always have been dangerous to watch (that is one of their fascinations), and sometimes the firemen bring their hazards with them. This 1858 illustration shows what happened to a Philadelphia dandy who failed to give the right of way to a passing fireman. *Historical Society of Pennsylvania*

Turning a Corner

(below) Graceful as a hook and ladder truck may be in skillful hands in a wide street, a narrow street will make for difficulties. Later models of truck had running boards for the firemen; and with a lower center of gravity, the vehicle was less likely to capsize on sharp curves.

A Rescue at the World *Fire* The rescue of Ida Small at the New York *World* Building fire.

could be pulled up by ropes to serve as a continuance of the other. But the fastening mechanism was not so permanent as planned; and after several collapses in mid-air, the firemen turned their red-shirted backs on this idea for a time. By the period of the Civil War, ladders of sixty-five or seventy-five feet in length were fairly common. But the raising of these heavy wooden devices was slow and difficult; several men had to "butt" the ladders on the ground to gain the necessary leverage. Daniel Hayes, who worked in the repair shop of the San Francisco Fire Department, thought up the idea of attaching the long ladder to a platform on the truck, with mechanical means being used to raise this ladder. In time, the raising process was handled by springs, compressed air, various chemicals, and electricity.

Technology was duly noted in a report to the National Association of Fire Engineers in Cleveland in 1878: "Whether 'aërial' ladders are less dangerous to their limbs and lives than will be the balloons which some enterprising inventor will before long feel constrained to originate for employment in reaching the ever increasing height of buildings, is an unsettled question."

It is only in the last few decades that metal ladders have come into use, and even today there are far more trucks with wooden aerial ladders than with aluminum or other metal alloys.

LESSONS OF THE *WORLD* BUILDING FIRE

At 10:12 A.M. on January 31, 1882, a fire broke out in the building of the New York *World*. This large structure occupied twelve city lots on Park Row, better known as "Newspaper Row" in that day. There was an instant rush by the 150 occupants of the edifice toward the stairs; but the flames got there first. Piles of newsprint in almost every corridor gave the fire fast-acting fuel, and most of the workers and visitors had to seek safety by way of the windows.

The ceilings were high, and the fire department's tallest ladders reached but to the third floor. The only aid that the firemen could give to persons on the fourth and fifth floors was to direct streams of

New York's First Scaling Ladder Rescue The St. George Flats were conspicuously advertised as strictly fireproof, but not at this fire in 1884. The elevator boy who had given the alarm was cut off from the stairs; ladders were too short; and the new scaling ladder bridged the gap from the five-story ladders to this seven-story ledge.

water into windows where people could be seen; beyond that, the trapped victims were on their own. Members of the Fire Patrol, the insurance salvage corps, attempted to catch several jumping persons in canvas waterproof covers, with indifferent success.

One spectacular rescue was that of Ida Small, who worked for the *World*. She calmly stood for ten minutes on a fourth floor ledge, in sight of the awed crowd, and watched efforts to rescue her. About six feet gaped between the top of the tallest ladder and her perch; ultimately she climbed down the back of a man balanced precariously on the top rung and was then carried to safety down the ladder.

Twelve persons perished in this half-million-dollar blaze. The effects of the conflagration on rescue methods was considerable. The fire commissioner, shocked at learning that ordinary methods no longer could be counted upon to rescue persons in structures more than seventy feet high, directed the chief to make recommendations to prevent a recurrence of this situation. The chief proposed that all hook and ladder companies should be equipped with scaling ladders and life lines.

The scaling ladder is a long rod of wood or metal, with a large hook at the top end; short crossbars are affixed to the rod. A fireman fastens the hook of the ladder to the window sill directly above him and then ascends to it; when he reaches this point, he unhooks the light ladder and fastens it to the window above his new perch. There is no practical limitation to the number of times that this operation can be repeated in order to make a rescue. This ladder received a very successful baptism of fire at the burning of the St. George Apartment House in New York in 1884. The tallest ladder would not reach a trapped man, but a fireman climbed two stories beyond the extension ladder to effect the rescue.

Other rescue devices that were perfected at about the same time were life belts (canvas girdles with large metal hooks that could be fastened to the rungs of a ladder, so that both hands were free to work), life nets (canvas or rope devices, originally known as "jumping sheets," into which a trapped person could leap), and life guns (which fired a projectile to which was fastened a cord, that could be used to pull rope up to a roof or inaccessible window).

THE WINDSOR HOTEL FIRE

Rapid communications systems, trained men, modern equipment, and the latest in rescue devices are magnificent protectors of life. But a burning edifice must be able to withstand fire long enough for people to get out, or to be saved.

If there had to be a hotel fire, no one could have asked for a better setup than the Windsor Hotel in New York. The blaze started at three o'clock in the afternoon on a warm, clear day. The surrounding streets were wide, particularly the broad Fifth Avenue, and the fire was discovered immediately. Moreover, half of the city's police were (literally) in the very front yard. Yet this was the worst hotel fire that New York City has experienced—so far.

On March 17, 1899, the annual St. Patrick's Day Parade took place on Fifth Avenue, and thousands of marchers and uncounted thousands of spectators filled the streets. So crowded were the sidewalks that some three hundred spectators sought a convenient vantage point in the Windsor Hotel. They, plus the hotel's 250 guests and about the same number of employees, pleasantly filled the building.

A guest threw a lighted match from the window on the Forty-sixth Street side of the building (precisely where the Colored Orphan Asylum had been burned during the Draft Riots in 1863), and the lovely lace curtains were ignited. The headwaiter saw the incident and tried to extinguish the flames. When he saw the task was beyond him, he sent a porter to notify the manager; then he dashed to the street to turn in a fire alarm. The alarm box, unfortunately, was on the other side of Fifth Avenue, and the police refused to let the headwaiter cross the line of march. His frantic explanations were ignored by a nonlistening policeman, who reprimanded him for jostling. Then a cloud of smoke swept out of the window, and a hundred voices screamed, "The Windsor's on fire!"

The alarm was sounded at 3:14 P.M., and three minutes later the first engine arrived. Within twenty minutes, a fifth alarm had been sent in.

The police commissioners happened to be passing the hotel in a carriage when the alarm was sounded and they attempted to organize police lines; but so great were the crowds that the fire horses had great difficulty in nearing the edifice.

Flames roared through the fine hotel with amazing rapidity. The fire crossed the top floor (a block long) in five minutes, as the famous wide halls, the tremendous stair wells, and the luxurious drapes of this magnificent hotel gave the blaze every opportunity. Firemen performed feats of prodigious

The Windsor Hotel Fire (right) These pictures of New York's worst hotel fire appeared after the tragedy in *Harper's Weekly*.

EARLY STAGE OF THE FIRE—RESCUING GUESTS.

THE FIRST PORTION OF THE FRONT WALL FALLING.

FALL OF SECOND PORTION OF FRONT WALL.

THE MAIN FRONT WALL FALLING.

Home of Miss Helen Gould where many of the Injured were taken.

THE NEXT MORNING—WATCHING FOR THE DEAD.

RESCUING GUESTS BY EXTENSION LADDERS.

bravery in rescuing guests, for the elevators and stairs were quickly useless. "Of the firemen who battled with that fierce blaze to save human life," declared the New York *Herald* of the following day, "there was not one who did not earn lasting tribute for deed and daring." Added the fire chief: "I doubt if what they accomplished there can ever be equaled."

Within an hour, the building was no more. A raging inferno left only the chimneys and parts of the outer wall standing. Fourteen bodies (persons who had jumped) were found in the streets; in all, ninety-two persons are believed to have perished in the blaze. The Windsor's loss was estimated to have been $1,000,000, with personal losses of the guests being set at $750,000.

In those days, the New York *Tribune* ran small advertisements at the bottom of page one. Perhaps through coincidence, perhaps through the make-up editor's sense of what was fitting, a small legend

appeared beneath the main story on the Windsor Hotel fire in the issue of the following day:

PORTABLE AUTOMATIC FIRE

ESCAPES. BABCOCK'S.

BALTIMORE'S FIRE OF 1904

At the start of the twentieth century, builders and landlords made much use of the proud phrase, "fireproof construction." The new buildings, it was said, were completely "safe"; no tenant had to be concerned about fire. Many persons wondered how "fireproof" a building really could be. Could the modern portion of a great city be ravaged by flames since the establishment of the new building codes?

At precisely 10:48 o'clock on the morning of Sunday, February 7, 1904, an automatic alarm box sounded its call from the basement of the Horst Building, located at the corner of German and Liberty streets and Hopkins Place in Baltimore. The structure was occupied by a wholesale drug com-

The Great Baltimore Fire A view of the great 1904 conflagration. The fire engines could have been from almost any of the communities located between Washington and New York.
Peale Museum, Baltimore

pany. Within forty-eight seconds, the first firemen arrived from a station two blocks away; and, because of the small size of the blaze, they attacked it with a single chemical line. But the cellar stock included some celluloid novelties, which exploded with tremendous force. The fire was thrust up an elevator shaft. Seven minutes later, an explosion fired the entire building.

A thirty-mile gale swept the flames through old and new buildings in the congested business area of Baltimore. Early during the battle, a cache of blasting powder was detonated with a tremendous roar. Businessmen quickly sensed that their offices and warehouses were doomed, and every express wagon in the city was hired to remove whatever property could be saved.

Fire Chief Horton was disabled by an electric shock from a fallen cable, but his assistants frantically summoned help from other communities. Engines were rushed from Wilmington, Washington, and Philadelphia. A detachment of nine steamers was sent by the New York Fire Department on railroad flatcars. But the out-of-town apparatus was greatly hampered by the distinctive hose couplings used in Baltimore. As a result, many of the borrowed smoke-eaters were obliged to pump water directly from the harbor. So great was the heat that some firemen fastened the nozzles of their hose lines to packing cases; then, the streams having been directed and fixed, the smoke-eaters took refuge in a convenient doorway. An unexpected hazard that the firemen had to face was liquor. The contents of 152 barrels of burning whisky flooded the streets, and three pieces of fire apparatus were destroyed as a result of this circumstance.

Martial law was declared. No one was allowed to cross military lines without a pass signed by the Attorney General of Maryland or by the president of the Baltimore Police Commissioners.

The fire officials decided to make one grand concentration against the main column of advancing flames. Engines were grouped to take advantage of natural obstacles presented by the waterfront and the stream Jones Falls. Here, with the help of a fireboat, the conflagration was checked.

Elsewhere, the fire seemed beyond the power of water to extinguish, and buildings had to be removed from the path of flames to create an area that the conflagration could not cross. Dynamite was used to level these structures.

This was the first great municipal fire since the introduction of "fireproof" buildings, and the nation watched the results with considerable interest.

Fire Escape A perilous escape was envisioned by the artist in 1881, but the scene might as well have been today. This is still the most common type of fire escape.

Actually few walls stood intact in the ravaged districts. Only four pillars were left of the Baltimore *Sun* Building, the first iron building to be erected in America. A principal lesson of the conflagration was that all openings in buildings of fireproof construction had to be protected against exterior attack. *Harper's Weekly* declared in an editorial: "The Baltimore fire showed what the great modern fires have shown before it, that the best of fire-proof buildings will melt away if there is enough fuel near them to make a sufficiently hot fire."

The conflagration lasted for a week. More than 140 acres were swept by the flames, and 2,500 buildings were destroyed, with losses of $100,000,000, of which $35,000,000 was estimated to have been covered by insurance. Only one life was lost.

The Winner At an 1878 competitive test in Waterloo, Iowa, this steamer won. Note the broom attached to the smokestack, indicative of the "clean sweep" that had been achieved. *American-LaFrance-Foamite Corporation*

Searchlight Wagon at Work (left bottom) A converted steamer serves as a searchlight wagon at a night fire in New York. The pumps and suction tubes, obviously, have been removed. *Ed. Waterman*

Snow Is a Fire Extinguisher When the wooden train of cars of the Hudson Railroad began to burn after this collision near Spuyten Duyvil, New York, in 1882, resourceful men rushed over these huge snowballs to blanket the flames. Fortunately this was before the days of electric locomotives.

Water Tower An early type of water tower used by the Rochester, New York, Fire Department. On most such pieces of apparatus, the tower when at rest leaned toward the rear rather than over the horses. Note the large amount of brass that must be carefully polished by someone. Time: June, 1908. *Peter Pirsch & Sons Co.*

Animal Ambulance This horse ambulance was used by the Boston Fire Department for the transportation of disabled animals. *Massachusetts Society for the Prevention of Cruelty to Animals*

SEAGRAVE TRUCK

Metal has replaced wood on most of today's extension ladders.

JOHN BEAN LADDER TRUCK

The ladders are concealed on this vehicle; they are withdrawn from the rear.

MACK COMBINATION

A ladder and other appurtenances of a hook and ladder company are carried by this pumper.

MACK LADDER TRUCK

Occasionally a community abandons the traditional red apparatus.

Study in Verticals Two water towers are hard at work at this fire in the Hoen Building in Baltimore in 1900. The numerous wires kept the extension ladder of the truck from reaching the walls. *Peale Museum, Baltimore*

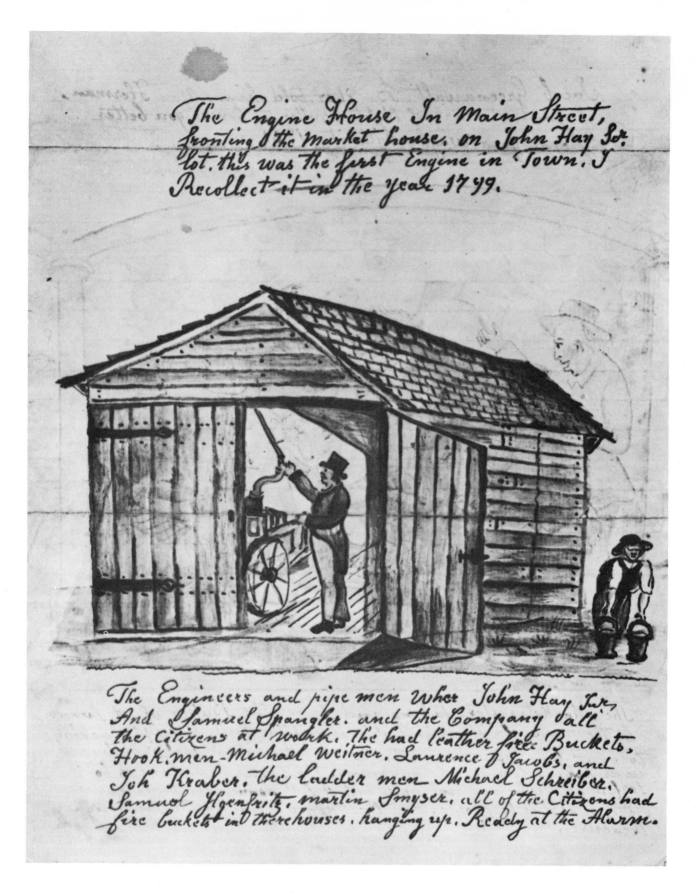

The Engine House In Main Street, fronting the market house, on John Hay Sr. lot. this was the first Engine in Town. I Recollect it in the year 1799.

The Engineers and pipe men wher John Hay Jr, And Samuel Spangler. and the Company all the Citizens at work. The had leather fire Buckets, Hook. men—Michael Weitner. Laurence Jacobs, and Joh Kraber, the ladder men—Michael Schreiber. Samuel Hoenfritz. martin Smyser. all of the Citizens had fire buckets in there houses. hanging up. Ready at the Alarm.

An Eighteenth-Century Firehouse

This water color was made by Lewis Miller to depict the first firehouse in York, Pennsylvania, as he remembered its appearance in 1799. York then maintained the requirement of having leather fire buckets on the walls of every home, hanging up, as Mr. Miller recalled, "Ready at the Alarm." *Historical Society of York County*

Firehouses and Pets

A chronicler of the old volunteers recalled that "the engine house was their sanctuary—their loved sanctuary—and no priest could have a greater regard for his than the firemen for theirs. The inducement must have been exceedingly strong to get the boys away from it."

The oldest firehouse in the United States was built of rough-hewn timbers and shingles near the center of the town of Mount Holly, New Jersey, in 1798. But the company which quartered its engine here was a veteran organization even at that time. It had been organized as the Britannia Fire Company of Bridgetown on July 11, 1752.

As the volunteer fire companies grew in numbers and in aggressiveness, their homes became clubhouses for the spirited members. There was little competition in beauty or spaciousness of the houses, however; there were other ways of settling questions of company superiority. But any true-blooded fireman contrived to spend as much time at the firehouse as possible so that, if an alarm were sounded, he would instantly be available for duty. Spare time was spent at the house; patriotic days were honored there; news of the day would be exchanged with the boys.

Of course there were duties as well. Even the simple engines such as hand pumpers had to be serviced, and Sunday morning was the customary cleaning time. This was when youths liked best to visit quarters, for the firemen, hard at "committee work," had plenty of time to relate their heroic episodes, with embellishments.

When the volunteers began to sleep at their firehouses in order to get a faster start to a night alarm, the houses became more elaborate. Some men merely slept under a buffalo robe on a plank floor, but other persons liked their creature comforts. Bunkrooms were set up in some houses that would have amazed the smoke-eaters of today. Lace pillows, lush carpets and drapes, ornate chandeliers, and oil paintings graced certain houses. Meeting rooms and social parlors were features of other buildings.

When firemen slept in quarters, a kitchen had to be available. Several companies became famous for the food they served. New York's Neptune Engine Company No. 6, which had been formed in 1765, was so renowned for its bean soup that the outfit was affectionately known as Old Bean Soup.

The Oldest Firehouse in America
This structure, built in 1798, still stands in Mount Holly, New Jersey. *Relief Fire Engine Co. No. 1, Mount Holly*

Cleaning the Machine (above) This 1851
Bufford lithograph shows a group of Boston firemen
cleaning their hand pumper. Note the torches on the
wall. *Library of Congress*

1856 Firehouse Dormitory (below) Hook
& Ladder Company No. 1 in New York had this elegant bunk room for its members. The men were not
so fastidious when fighting flames or firemen.

Eagle Hose Company No. 1 of that city was renowned for its mutton pies; and if an alarm were received during a repast, the men would gulp down their unfinished pies while running to the fire, an accomplishment which gained these smoke-eaters the designation of Mutton Hose Company.

Firehouses were sometimes given over to "open house" when funds were being raised for charity, or when a new engine had been acquired, or when distinguished "visiting firemen" from other communities were expected. But generally the quarters were not open to the public, as befitted a club. Visitors were restricted to the ground floor.

When persons were dislodged by fire, they knew they could find shelter, food, and sometimes clothing at the nearest firehouse. Negroes who were pursued by mobs during New York's frightful Draft Riot in 1863 were assured of sanctuary if they could but reach a fire station.

The advent of the horse changed the interior architecture of firehouses. At first the animals were kept in stalls in a yard behind the house; but much time was lost in opening stable and rear firehouse doors to let the animals reach the engines when an alarm was sounded. As time became more important, stalls were placed on a rear side of the apparatus floor of the firehouse itself; but valuable moments were lost when the animals had to back out of their stalls and then wheel to the front. So the stalls were placed at the back of the house, with doors that enabled the horses to reach the equipment without turning.

A 1791 Firehouse The firehouse of Engine Company No. 13, New York City, as it appeared when the company was formed in 1791. Pine dating back to that time was used for the purpose, and old records were carefully checked as to details. The original firehouse stood in Maiden Lane, and the reconstruction also is in Maiden Lane, in The Home Insurance Company office. The engine itself was built by James Smith around 1800. *H. V. Smith Museum of The Home Insurance Company*

By the 1880's, brass sliding poles were in general use. Previously the men had to stumble downstairs from their sleeping quarters when a night alarm was received, or else they slept on an extension of the apparatus floor, beyond the horses. Thanks to the sliding pole, firemen could have their own dormitory floor above the apparatus, which could be reached in a few seconds by way of a hole in the ceiling. A few companies had special chutes that connected the driver's bed with his seat on the apparatus on the floor below.

Old-time firehouses were usually three stories high. The first floor was for apparatus and horses; the second floor was the dormitory for the men; the third floor was for feed storage and for "sundry" equipment, such as a pool table. There are still many firehouses in use where there may be seen an iron arm extending from a third floor window facing the street. This was a hoist for bales of hay for the horses. Today's firehouses, thanks to better design, are frequently two stories in height.

Well into the twentieth century, many firehouses had living accommodations for the wives and children of married smoke-eaters. In those days, a fireman was supposed to be available for duty most of the time; thus his family could share his quarters. There are men in the New York Fire Department today who were born in firehouses when that arrangement was still in effect.

In the day of the fire horse, the steeds were the principal pets. The firemen loved their horses, fed them dainties, and taught them tricks. People of the neighborhood rendered whatever favors were possible. A daily visit to see the fire horses was part of the routine of countless persons.

The Alarm (right) Everyone moves swiftly in the firehouse when the apparatus is to roll. Even Spot, the company Dalmatian, is making fast time. *Mine Safety Appliance Company*

Fire Horses at Rest A very unusual photograph of the same three black horses that may be seen pulling Engine 219's steamer on page 183. The picture is unusual in that the alert steeds are all lying down at the same time. Every sound of a bell had these animals (figuratively) on their toes, and it took the photographer four hours of patient vigil before he could perpetuate this scene. *Ed. Waterman*

Before, during, and after the reign of the horse, there were the fire dogs. Major, of Mechanics Hose Company No. 47 in New York, loved the life of a smoke-eater to such an extent that when the volunteers were disbanded, he joined Engine Company No. 3 of Elizabeth, New Jersey. Rollo, of Metamora Hose Company No. 29 in New York, frequently upheld his company's honor in combat with other fire dogs. Ponto, a liver and white pointer in St. Louis' volunteer days, would rouse his sleeping master when an alarm was sounded; then the dog would race him to the firehouse. Sparky, a wire-haired terrier that rode to fires in Norfolk, Virginia, liked to pull the engine bell rope with his teeth. Pooch, of Engine Company No. 13 in Nashville, Tennessee, was on twenty-four-hour duty and invariably traveled to fires on the appara-

tus; immediately after maternity, she had to be locked in a room to keep her from deserting her puppies in favor of an alarm.

The dogs learned, or were taught, many tricks. In New York alone, these dogs have left their marks in the record books: Dan, of Engine Company No. 14, would "drop dead" when a toy pistol was fired. Barney, of Engine Company No. 25, cleared absent-minded persons from the street when his apparatus responded to an alarm; the driver said that his horses showed increased speed when Barney led the way, for they confidently knew that the road would be clear. Cappy, of Engine Company No. 65, once aroused his fellow denizens at the Speyer Animal Hospital by barking frantically; then a fire was discovered on the next block. One day that same dog failed to re-

A Firehouse in the Olden Days   Many an oldster will recall this scene with nostalgic pleasure. It could have been the door of any firehouse in the country on a warm summer day, but actually it shows the Lincoln, Illinois, Fire Department in 1905. The chain was to keep horses from wandering out; it was not supposed to keep young enthusiasts from wandering in. *Illinois State Historical Library*

Spot Clears the Way

(left) More than seventy years ago, a fire dog on active duty. The animal, not knowing where the fire is until he actually sees it, may be embarrassed by having the engine turn into a side street without warning; then he will have to veer about and go into high gear until he can overtake the steamer.

A fire dog's historic function was to clear the street before the onrushing horses. That day is past, but many fire dogs are more than ornamental today. They "roll" to the blaze on the apparatus; at a fire, they do guard duty and may refuse to let anybody but a fireman remove equipment from the rig. Some dogs do not leave quarters but prevent pilferage when the firemen are out on duty. Other animals help the house watchman relieve the tedium of his otherwise lonely vigil on desk duty.

He is a very rare fireman who does not love the company mascot. Others in the community are likewise sympathetic to the animals. When Dell, the Dalmatian of Engine Company No. 4 in Newark, New Jersey, became too old for active service, the Newark *News* printed an appeal for a younger dog. Upon the serious illness of Smoky of Fire Company No. 3 in Irvington, New Jersey, two Dalmatians from other companies provided blood for transfusions.

Chaplain's Dog

The most popular fire dogs were Dalmatians; but dogs of any (or no) breed performed their services. Chaplain Handel of the New York Fire Department proudly shows his English bull terrier. *Ed. Waterman*

spond to a pier fire on the hose car as usual; when the vehicle was destroyed at that fire, the men were sure that Cappy had displayed uncanny "dog-sense." Boots, of Hook & Ladder Company No. 16, would roll over a lighted cigarette on the floor, to snuff the fire, but if anyone dropped an unlighted cigarette to tease the dog, the animal responded only with a dirty look.

New York had other fire animals. Barney, of Engine Company No. 59, was a cat that learned how to use a sliding pole. Another cat, Nigger, of Engine Company No. 65, rode to fires on the engine and lost one of its lives when he was buried by a floor collapse. Jenny, a monkey attached to Hook & Ladder Company No. 20, would obey orders from a chief but from no one else; the firemen presumed that she had given herself the title and rank of a captain, responsible only to a chief.

Eagle Insurance Company

This marker was issued by a Cincinnati organization in about 1855. *Insurance Company of North America*

Fire Association of Philadelphia

A primitive wooden hydrant graces this marker.

Associated Firemen's Insurance Company

A fireman equipped with speaking trumpet and hydrant wrench, about 1851. *Insurance Company of North America*

Role of the Insurance Companies

It was quickly realized in the American colonies that the tragic losses at fires could be mitigated only in part by the firemen. The loss of wealth in what was not a wealthy community constituted a grave problem.

One approach to this problem was taken by the Massachusetts Charitable Fire Society, which was incorporated in 1794 "for the purpose of relieving such as may suffer by fire, and of stimulating genius to useful discoveries tending to secure the lives and property of their fellow men from destruction by that element." Paul Revere was one of the most active men in the formation of this society. The group examined machines and inventions for the extinguishment of fire; but most of the good deeds were in helping the people whose homes had been burned out. As a Society poet laureate declared,

So when all sweeping fire extends,
From here the rescuing hand of bounty bends.

In 1693, William Penn had suggested after a bad fire that public subscription be made to compensate people for fire losses. The first fire insurance company in America was started in Charleston, South Carolina, but the venture was short-lived. On April 13, 1752, the second company opened its doors: the Philadelphia Contributorship For The Insurance Of Houses From Loss By Fire, which is in business today. Benjamin Franklin was one of the original directors of this company, which frequently was called the Hand-in-Hand Insurance

Company because of the cartouche of helping hands that was used. In 1784, the Mutual Insurance Company of Philadelphia was formed. The Philadelphia Contributorship would not insure houses that were close to trees, as the fire hazard was believed excessive; there was also believed to be a danger to tree-sheltered houses from lightning, and who in the world of that day knew more about lightning than Director Franklin? The Mutual Insurance Company, however, was willing to insure such shaded homes, and the company's insignia was therefore a flourishing tree.

Mutual Assurance Company
The "flowering tree" fire mark dates back to 1784. *The Mutual Assurance Company for Insuring Houses from Loss by Fire*

Insurance Protection in the Eighteenth Century

This engraving, made in the eighteenth century, shows a fire in New York. Just about everything pertinent to fire fighting in that day may be found in the picture. Note, at the extreme right, members of the Hand-in-Hand Fire Company, who are using bags to take property from the burning structure to a place of greater safety. *I. N. Phelps Stokes Collection, New York Public Library*

Pennsylvania Fire Mark

Insurance plate used to distinguish properties insured by the Germantown Mutual Fire Insurance Company. *Germantown Fire Insurance Company.*

164

Insurance Company of North America
This fire mark (the second type used by the company) was instituted in 1796. *Insurance Company of North America*

An Early Fire Mark
This particular fire mark was issued in 1760 by the Philadelphia Contributorship in connection with its policy No. 506. *Philadelphia Contributorship*

Baltimore Equitable Fire Mark
Fire mark issued in 1794, with the early policy number (38) indicated upon it. The clasped iron hands were mounted on wood. *Baltimore Equitable Society*

The fire insurance companies insured the property of their members from loss by fire; but the work of these companies did not stop there. They endeavored to reduce fire losses in various ways. A French visitor to Philadelphia in the last decade of the eighteenth century recorded how insurance company men came to all fires to encourage the volunteer firemen to greater efforts. The encouragement was not only vocal. Several insurance companies offered rewards to the first firemen to reach the fire, or to those smoke-eaters who would fight the flames in any building that was covered by the particular insurance company. However laudable the motivation for the rewards may have been, the results were less than satisfactory. Desire to capture the prize money caused many brawls between fire companies as to who should reach the scene of the conflagration first; or the first company to arrive, lest it have to share the reward, would refuse oft-needed help from later arrivals. The reward for quenching a fire in an insured building produced a condition in some communities under which the firemen simply would not waste their energies on any uninsured building.

BUNK ROOM.

N.Y. INSURANCE PATROL.

AT A FIRE.

In the days when any building reached by the flames was considered as lost, it was necessary for some firemen to decide where to concentrate their efforts. Thus many insurance companies placed metal plates, or insurance marks, upon buildings covered by policies. The marks had two main purposes: (1) to show the smoke-eaters which buildings were insured; that meant that rewards might be anticipated; (2) to show would-be arsonists that the owner of the property would be reimbursed for any loss, so there was no reason to try to ruin him maliciously.

The Philadelphia Contributorship ordered its first fire marks on May 20, 1752, when the company was only five weeks old.

Fire marks remained in use in many communities until the establishment of the professional fire departments, which were not concerned with the question of whether a property was covered by insurance. But at least one company, the Baltimore Equitable, still issues its insurance plate (a reasonable facsimile of its 1794 marker) to any policyholder who desires it.

Fire insurance companies frequently helped the smoke-eaters by offering rewards for the apprehension and conviction of persons who had set fires. Some insurance executives recognized their own responsibility as to arson. "Overinsurance," said the president of the Continental Insurance Company in 1878, "is a great provocation to incendiarism."

Another service of the insurance companies was the protection of property from damage by fire, smoke, water, and theft. In 1780, the Hand-in-Hand Fire Insurance Company was formed in New York, and eight years later the preamble to its regulations declared: "The utility of associations for the purpose of avoiding as much as possible the ruinous consequences which may occasionally happen by fire induced a number of individuals to form themselves into select companies, with the laudable view of affording their particular aid to each other, and to the community at large." Not only were these men volunteers, but they had to supply their own tools. Each member of the company was required to provide himself with two bags, made of 2½ yards of raven's duck, equipped with proper strings and marked with the owner's name and "H.H." At fires, these men would remove to safety in their capacious bags anything that was both burnable and portable. And to see that thieves did not invade a gutted structure, members of the group would be posted at the scene, with orders to see that no one entered the premises without giving the secret password.

Another early group of this nature was the Mutual Assistance Bag Company, which was formed in New York in 1803. Many early pictures of fires show the insurance men carrying bags of valuables to safe quarters. But some persons had wicked

STORAGE ROOM

SAVING GOODS

I. PRANISHNIKOF

The Fire Patrol in Action Fire Patrol No. 1 in Murray Street, New York, gets ready to roll to a fire in 1876. The border pictures indicate the function of the insurance men: saving property from damage by flames, smoke, and water. Later the firehouse was equipped with brass sliding poles for faster arrival of the men on the apparatus floor.

ideas as to where the bags would be taken. Even today, there are those who unwarrantedly refer to the insurance corps men as "the forty thieves."

In the larger communities, the fire insurance companies collectively maintained a group of salvage men, who would protect property in burning structures regardless of whether the premises were insured; in fact, the salvage crew rarely even knew at the time who the insurer (if any) was. The Fire Patrol in New York was started by the insurance underwriters in 1839. The first employees were men who had other positions during the daytime but who patrolled the streets, looking for fires, at night. By the 1840's, a light wagon was being used by the patrol to transport protective covers to night fires. The vehicle was stored in an upper floor of a building used by insurance men; but at seven o'clock each evening, the vehicle was lowered to the street by ropes, to be available for instant service.

In St. Louis, a group known as "The Fire Wardens" was formed in 1844 for the purpose of protecting property at fires.

In Boston, two insurance agents in 1849 procured canvas bags, each of which contained three small oilcloth covers. Upon an alarm, an assistant engineer would draft anyone he could find to go to the blaze and place covers over property that might be harmed by smoke or water. By 1858, the hook and ladder companies were provided with protective covers, to be applied by the firemen "when not engaged in their regular duties." In ten years, the Boston Protective Department was formed of men who were paid to look after the safety of property at fires; an old milk wagon was the first vehicle used.

In time, special crews to look after property were established by insurance underwriters as a group in the larger communities. A variety of names was used for these departments, such as the salvage corps, fire patrol, insurance corps, or insurance patrol. Salvage covers range in size from 9 x 12 feet to 14 x 18 feet, and trucks today can carry from forty to a hundred covers. The men of these companies enter burning structures with the

Philadelphia Salvage Men Fire Insurance Patrol No. 2 of Philadelphia. The apparatus resembles a hose cart. *Philadelphia Fire Insurance Patrol*

WARD LA FRANCE PUMPER

Short ladders are borne by this particular engine.

AMERICAN LA FRANCE TRUCK

The driver rides in front of the engine on this late-model extension truck.

SEAGRAVE PUMPER

Fire-fighting tools are carried in cabinets at the side.

AMERICAN LA FRANCE PUMPER

Note the complex system of valves and controls.

firemen, to place covers over property that might be damaged by water, smoke, or other hazards. Other protective equipment that is carried on the trucks includes tar paper and roofing nails (to protect property from storm damage if roof or walls have been injured); squeegees, brooms, and sawdust to be used in removing excess water; sprinkler heads to be used as replacements for water-gushing sprinkler pipes. Sometimes portable pumps are carried to rid a structure of accumulated water.

Another function historically engaged in by the fire insurance companies is the introduction of improved fire-fighting equipment. It was the insurance companies that encouraged the development of the Hodge steamer in 1840, and the underwriters

Insurance Patrol An early type of equipage used by the New York fire insurance companies to protect property at fires. This hand-drawn vehicle was referred to as a "pie wagon." It contained protective coverings.

Horseless Carriage The Chicago Fire Insurance Patrol purchased this Woods Electric car in 1907. After several months of use, the vehicle was discarded. *Chicago Fire Insurance Patrol*

gave New York its first steamer in 1859. By that year, St. Louis' underwriters had provided two steamers. A large part of the cost of Cincinnati's second steamer was provided by the insurance men.

As the insurance companies became conscious of the public education phase of their profession, advice was given to fire departments in a variety of fields. Organizations such as the National Board of Fire Underwriters in time gave advice on such questions as equipment, organization, and business methods. After disastrous fires, the insurance companies would help a community to reorganize a fire department that had been found wanting. The companies even made recommendations based upon special studies, such as the adequacy of a community's fire equipment to cope with the specific hazards that were to be faced.

The insurance companies were usually progressive in their own protective equipment. The New York Fire Patrol was using horses to pull its apparatus before the fire department reached this technological development. In the winter of 1874–75, when severe storms destroyed the fire alarm telegraph wires in New York, the fire department stationed men on foot in various parts of the city to look for fires; but the Fire Patrol used mounted horsemen (known as "The Cowboys") to cover the community. The Boston Protective Department and also the Chicago Fire Insurance Patrol independently pioneered in the use of automotive equipment in 1907, long before most fire departments even thought of the idea.

Working relations between the firemen and the insurance salvage corps men are harmonious today, but such was not always the case. The volunteer smoke-eaters deeply resented the efforts of the insurance underwriters to introduce steamers and professional fire departments, and this resentment was taken out (often physically) upon the fire patrolmen, who were regarded as representatives of the obnoxious insurance interests. Even after paid fire departments had been installed, the insurance corps men were sometimes suspected of being spies who would report to their powerful employers concerning firemen or techniques that were inefficient. For several years after the introduction of

the professional firemen, it was not unusual to hear a smoke-eater cry that call of the old volunteers, "Throw the red caps out!" (The insurance patrolmen usually had red helmets, to distinguish them from the black-helmeted firemen.)

Today the salvage corps men work side by side with the firemen in every way. The magazine of the New York Fire Department, *WNYF*, devotes the same relative space to the news and obituaries of the Fire Patrol as it does to departmental news.

MILWAUKEE'S NEWHALL HOUSE

The warnings of insurance men as to the safety of a building are not always heeded. But if the insurance companies will not touch a structure, the fire companies all too frequently will have to do so. A case in point was the Newhall House in Milwaukee, a famous hotel in its day. But that day was long past by 1883. The six stories were largely of wood; yet what made the building so potentially dangerous was the system of intricate passages that converted the upper hallways into a maze. Two fire escapes were generally considered as inadequate for the population of the hotel.

So many fires had occurred in the old building that local agents refused to handle insurance upon the premises. A Milwaukee newspaper editor "had looked upon it as doomed if it ever got on fire in the night."

On the night of January 9, 1883, more than three hundred guests and employees retired. They were rudely awakened at four o'clock the next morning, when frantic shrieks announced that the dreadful peril had materialized. Flames and smoke made the corridors all but impenetrable. Numerous persons stumbled past exits without finding them. No one appeared to take charge or to assert any authority.

When the firemen arrived, every window in the hotel seemed to be filled by an imploring person. Because of a forest of telegraph wires outside of the structure, the firemen could not raise any tall ladders. Some guests were rescued when firemen made a ladder bridge across an alley from the roof of a neighboring structure. Frantic people jumped from their windows toward life nets held by the smoke-eaters; but, in many instances, the leaping persons became entangled in the telegraph wires.

Milwaukee was excited as it never was before,
On learning that the fire bells all around
Were ringing to eternity a hundred souls
*   or more,*
*   And the Newhall House was burning to the*
*   ground.*

Hotel Fire in Milwaukee On the night of January 10, 1883, many lives were lost when the Newhall House in Milwaukee, Wisconsin, was devoured by flames. The overhead telegraph wires impeded proper use of ladders for rescue work.

The San Francisco Fire A general view of the San Francisco fire of 1906. *California Historical Society*

In 1905, as a result of the Great Baltimore Fire of the previous year, the National Board of Fire Underwriters made a study of the adequacy of municipal fire protection services, and several cities were warned that their facilities were not up to standard. One of the communities thus warned was San Francisco. But the warning was not heeded in time. On April 18, 1906, the fifty-two square miles of the city were protected only by sixty-two engine companies and fifteen hook and ladder companies.

At five-thirteen o'clock on that morning, an earthquake took place. A rumble as of thunder was heard far below the surface of the ground; the city quivered, while great cracks appeared in roadways. Massive steel and stone buildings swayed; less substantial structures collapsed. Five minutes after the first convulsion, a second one occurred. The quakes were not of catastrophic importance, but a number of fires was started. These doubtless could have been held in check, except for the fact that the three main water lines to Crystal Springs Lake had been broken. Without water, the most minor fires became infernos, and most of the downtown portions of the city were ablaze as helpless property owners stood watching.

The firemen, although they could do little to quench the flames, were anything but idle. They plunged into the remains of buildings and hunted alertly for the living and the dead. Three hundred bodies were recovered by ten o'clock that morning.

By midmorning, Federal troops sent by General Funston were patrolling the streets to preserve order. Looters were shot, and civilians administered their own rough justice to any thief they detected. The police entered food stores to see that no person bought too much. Horses that were required by the authorities were commandeered, sometimes at pistol point. Automobiles, although not yet used as fire engines, were employed to transport firemen from one assignment to another.

Block after block had to be evacuated as large zones of the city became seas of flames. Dozens of communities rushed in reinforcements of men and apparatus, but the lack of water at vital points was fatal. Flames could be checked only when they came within pumping distance of the bay or some other body of water. Fires could only be isolated, not extinguished.

An unusually determined stand was made before buildings that just *couldn't* be lost. After a terrific battle, the United States Mint was saved by a force of men under the command of a former chief of the Oakland Fire Department.

Not until the third day of the conflagration was the fire brought under control. At Van Ness Avenue, a space was cleared five hundred feet wide and nearly a mile long to serve as a firebreak. Buildings were dynamited without hesitation; and when the ruins seemed to offer a lodging place for flames, large-caliber guns from San Francisco's forts were used to shoot point-blank into the debris. A tremendous force of fire fighters was assembled here; for if the fire could not be checked at this point, the entire city was doomed. Some mains had been repaired by the time the main body of the fire reached this locality, and steamers in relays pumped brine from San Francisco Bay. But this defense line held for ten hours, and then this phase of the battle was over.

No city ever had experienced such a catastrophe in peacetime. About 75 per cent of San Francisco was in ruins. Some four square miles of the city had been ravaged, covering three thousand acres. About 28,000 buildings were lost on 520 city blocks, and the total loss estimates were as high as $500,-000,000. Homeless were 300,000 people. Among the 452 persons killed was Fire Chief Sullivan, who died early in the battle.

174

Fire Horses

Any mention of the Old Days in the fire department is apt to conjure up the picture of mighty horses with flying hooves and manes. Thus it is strange to note how difficult it was for horses to get into the fire departments in the first place.

In the early days, when fire fighting was a fiercely competitive activity, the men liked to think that human muscle was the chief ingredient not only in extinguishing fires but in reaching the scene of the conflagration. Besides, there was the economic factor: manpower was free, but who would supply the horses and pay for their upkeep? Men were cheaper than animals. In that day, buildings were relatively low, and engines accordingly were small and light, easily pulled by men. On at least one occasion, even an aged Negress was able to pull Oceanus' pumper to a New York fire unassisted.

At the beginning of the nineteenth century, the Good Will Fire Company of Philadelphia experimented with the use of horses to pull equipment, despite the ribald comments of men of other companies. It was not until 1830 that the first New York company made use of a horse: Hook and Ladder Company No. 1 used a single animal, which was disgraced when the company was passed en route to a fire by the crack men of Engine Company No. 11. It was said that the horse was never the same after that experience, nor were the embarrassed boys of No. 11 Engine. Matthew Armstrong, who was a runner with Engine Company No. 29 in New York, owned a horse named Skinny that sometimes galloped to fires on its own account, for the sport; and on several occasions the steed was used to help out when the "masheen" got stuck in the mud. But when New York had a cholera epidemic in the 1830's, the shortage of men made the use of horses a necessity for a time.

The *Morning Courier and New York Enquirer* of September 26, 1836 declared that "horses should assuredly be immediately used for conveying the engines to a fire. We learn that in London the fire engine is placed ready for use in a vehicle, to which horses standing in a stable close by are immediately attached on an alarm of fire, and it is strange that so obvious an advantage should not be introduced here."

But the volunteer firemen liked to run with their engines. Horses were used to pull the apparatus in parades; but when there was a real emergency, manpower was more reliable. At least the firemen liked to believe that such was the case.

It was the related events of the invention of the steamer and the passing of the volunteers that brought the horse into active fire service. The original steamers were too heavy for manual propulsion, and the Cincinnati pioneers vacillated between self-propelled engines and horse-drawn apparatus. In time the horses proved more dependable.

As apparatus became heavier and as communities spread over more territory, horses became the rule rather than the exception. The professional fire departments made them standard equipment.

The first horse-drawn equipment, steamers and also hook and ladder trucks, had no space for the driver, who rode astride a horse in the manner of a horse artilleryman.

Going to the Fire This painting of a small-sized steamer was made by R. A. Fox and J. A. Fraser, Jr. in 1885. *Insurance Company of North America*

The smaller communities at first made use of any horse that was available when an alarm was sounded. Sometimes livery stables or business houses were under contract to send animals to the firehouse when an alarm was sounded; other localities called upon the municipal stables to send around any horses not being used at the moment for hauling, street cleaning, or other service. But in the cities and larger towns, the well-trained animals were fabulously skilled in their profession. The horses were kept in stalls at the rear of the firehouse or, occasionally, in a stable to the rear of the firehouse. Harness was suspended over the wagon shaft by an automatic iron hanger. When the alarm sounded, springs released the stall doors or chains, and the horses almost spontaneously appeared under their individual harnesses, which dropped instantly when the driver seized the reins. Meanwhile the house watchman snapped the special collars, and automatic weights attached to little pulleys on the ceiling carried the framework that had held the harness out of the way. The collars could be fastened around the horses' necks very rapidly; some special collars could be fastened in less than a second.

But long after the larger fire departments had adopted the horse, many smaller communities hesitated. An observer in Paterson, New Jersey, noted in 1888 that "the question of the use of horses was an ever-fresh topic of discussion amongst the fire-

men as it was generally supposed that a paid force would follow close upon the heels [sic] of the horses." Yet these volunteer firemen were willing to accept progress and even to pay for it; the men of Engine Company No. 1 purchased at their own expense a team of bays to haul the steamer.

Despite certain obvious disadvantages of sharing a house with horses, the smoke-eaters almost to a man enthusiastically accepted the working partnership. A wonderful sense of camaraderie arose. The same dangers were shared and the same discomforts. Thus pictures of great blizzards and floods show man and beast struggling side by side to pull the apparatus to a fire. The New York *Herald* of March 14, 1888, thus reported the Great Blizzard: "When firemen dragged their engines to fires it looked as if they were soldiers hurrying cannon through the wilderness as they sat on their horses laboring the leaders and following the dim figures of mounted scouts in the mad tempest." Firemen were obliged to commandeer any carriage or truck horses they encountered to help the fire horses pull apparatus through the drifts.

A New York battalion chief recalled that "each company took pride in its own quarters, its equipment, its officers and men. But most of all, in its *horses.*" The men not only respected their courageous, willing, hard-working equine companions; they became fiercely fond of them. The secretary of the New York Fire Department wrote in 1907: "Great is the fire-horse and mighty is his master's love and respect for him. . . . No horses in the world are treated better than the fire-horses." The animals were carefully curried and combed; their hooves were oiled and sometimes painted black. Many cities had a ceremonial "bedding in" of the horses at eight o'clock each evening. The steeds were the darlings, not only of the firemen, but of the children of the neighborhood; and many adults made a point of bringing lumps of sugar every time they passed a firehouse.

Some of the fire horses developed highly personal characteristics. In New York City alone, these animals have left themselves a name: Big Jim of Hook & Ladder Company No. 23, when thirsty, could release the lock on his stall, walk to the sink, and open the faucet with his teeth. Baby, a steel gray of Engine Company No. 2, would crawl *under* the chain barring his stall if the mechanism didn't work quickly enough; he also was an inveterate hand-shaker. Dick of Engine Company No. 18 would release the harness over his position if the house watchman were too slow. Roger of Engine Company No. 21 was so well trained that he was allowed to wander unattended in the street. Major of Engine Company No. 14 would cough delicately when questioned about his health. Bull of Engine Company No. 39 refused to let any fireman get on the hose wagon until he (Bull) was hitched.

A Match In the larger fire departments, efforts frequently were made to match the horses in a particular span or team as to size, color, and general appearance. The dappled grays attached to the steamer are as well matched as the chestnut horses drawing the water tower. The scene is Madison Square, New York, where Fifth Avenue and Broadway cross. *New-York Historical Society*

The horses seemed to sense the importance and excitement of their jobs. "Nothing so disgusts a horse as delay after he has done his duty in getting under a harness," it was recorded in 1894. Many animals seemed to be able to count the strokes on the alarm bell and to recognize the box numbers to which they responded: for example, a steed might only get excited when there was sounded an alarm beginning with four taps of the bell. Such a horse, when transferred to another company, would get frantic when the firemen paid no attention to a signal beginning with four taps of the bell.

The drivers were even more fond of their animals than were the other firemen, if that was possible. Some drivers risked having charges filed against them for slow response to an alarm, rather than report that their beloved horses were getting too old for active fire service. A Detroit fire horse named Maggie became generally known as Maggie Scott, Scott being the surname of her driver. Fire chiefs were assigned a buggy with driver, but many chiefs preferred to handle the reins themselves. There were examples of horses, when retired for age or injury, that were purchased at great financial sacrifice by the firemen who had loved them.

Frequently horse shows or exhibitions would have special classes for fire horses, and many fire horses were so well cared for and trained that they could compete against any steeds in their weight classification.

The speed with which a crack team could get the apparatus rolling is almost unbelievable today. In 1896, the steeds of Engine Company No. 1 in New York would have their steamer in the street fourteen seconds after the alarm was received. It was not at all unusual for apparatus to be rolling within eighteen seconds of the alarm. So rapid were the horses that when automobiles were first placed in the same quarters, the animals got to the fire first. It was only after the self-starter was installed that automobiles could reach the fire before the horses.

During the first visit of the Grand Duke Alexis of Russia to New York in 1871, an alarm was sounded for his benefit four blocks from the nearest firehouse. In two minutes and thirty-five seconds, the horses had been hitched up, the steamer had

Horse Power and Man Power (above) Early horse-drawn fire apparatus could carry only those men who had work to do en route to fires, such as drivers and stokers. Thus these trumpet-carrying officers probably couldn't use the trumpets for some minutes after reaching the scene of the fire.

The Blizzard of 1888 (right) Even today, a heavy storm is apt to require all off-duty firemen to return to their quarters. In New York's Great Blizzard of '88, snow was a tremendous peril, and firemen had to help the horses pull the heavy equipment through clogged streets.

been pulled through traffic to the firebox, and a stream of water was pumped upon a designated building. Improved horse collars in later years could have speeded up this time.

Residents of a neighborhood often took great personal pride in the appearance and performance of the local fire horses. Sometimes the animals were rewarded for a job well done. The horses of Engine Company No. 14 in New York were given special harness by the Huyler Candy Company after an eighteen-hour factory fire.

Some firemen might object to the chore of cleaning the horses after a hard night's battle with the flames, or they might complain about the inevitable sounds and odors; but most of the smoke-eaters fully appreciated their working partners. O. Henry, in "The Trimmed Lamp," well reflected the feelings peculiar to each fire company when he spoke of "Erebus and Joe, the finest team in the whole department—according to the crew of 99."

Fast Time in Elizabeth, New Jersey
Fire apparatus thunders down Main Street in this New Jersey community in about 1880. The engineer on the rear platform of the steamer looks a bit unprofessional in a derby but he seems to have been quite professional in getting the boiler fired. Also discernible in this painting by E. Opper is a chief, who is driving his own buggy. *Rhode Island School of Design, Providence, R.I.*

All in Step (right) A New Haven, Connecticut, steamer rushes to the fray. It is related that a newspaper photographer sought to get Yale student Robert Taft to pose in 1912, but Taft said that he lacked time. The disappointed photographer then used his film on the gallant steeds; and when he returned to his dark room, he discovered that the derby-wearing Taft had managed to pose after all. No one was too busy to watch the engines clatter past. *Brown Brothers*

A Gallery of
Fire Horses in Action

There were few concepts in the Greek mythology so appealing as Pegasus, the celebrated flying horse. Interpretations of this theme appear on Carthaginian coins. Spenser, Shakespeare, Pope, Burns, Morris, Schiller, Longfellow, and other poets have written of the sheer beauty and power of this winged steed. But only Schiller thought enough in our modern idiom to translate the gigantic concept of the flying horse into everyday usage. He wrote "Pegasus in Harness."

The education of the horse into the fire horse presents the theme of the winged steed in the most glorious hues. The frantic hauling of a bulky, steaming boiler or a grotesquely elongated series of ladders through city streets toward some rapidly disintegrating structure scarcely suggests a stirring picture that would excite the hearts of men for generations. But the fire horses actually were able to recreate this idea of Pegasus, the flying steed. Absent were the trappings of the rider Bellerophon, or the lovely fountains on Mount Olympus where the fabulous animal refreshed itself. The gallant fire horses were nonetheless just as picturesque as the steed which lived in Zeus' palace, and they were far more useful than any mythological creature.

On the following pages are presented photographs that show relatively modern reincarnations of Pegasus, the flying horse. Bellerophon never was able to master his steed, nor was Schiller's poet-turned-cartman able to drive Pegasus. But the firemen here shown were able to master their great animals or, at least, seemingly to fly with them toward battle against their common foe.

Charge! A well-matched team of white chargers dashes through the streets of Portland, Oregon, early in the twentieth century. *Les. T. Ordeman*

Engine Company No. 10, F.D.N.Y.

(above) Note the distended nostrils of the straining horses as the steamer rushes to a fire. But however winded the animals became, they were always good for that last sprint to the fire. *Brown Brothers*

Engine Company No. 219, F.D.N.Y.

(below) The informal appearance of the firemen suggests a small town's volunteer fire brigade, but actually this is Engine Company No. 219 of the New York Fire Department. The summer heat is responsible for these smoke-eaters' nonchalant attire. *Ed. Waterman*

Fast Time (above) The drama has been heightened by the fact that the steam whistle added its cloud to that of the smokestack. These beauties are galloping just south of Seventy-second Street on Broadway, New York City. *Brown Brothers*

Speed in Buffalo (below) Engine Company No. 13 of the Buffalo Fire Department is proceeding right smartly at some time in the 1890's. But if one merely looks at the wheels, the steamer seems to be standing still. *Buffalo Historical Society*

Eager for the Fray (above) Hook & Ladder Company No. 8 about 1910. It is located in the heart of New York City's warehouse and shipping areas. The huge horses could virtually make their own way in traffic. *Brown Brothers*

Clear the Way! (below) This Juggernaut virtually flies over the unpaved streets. The company commander and his engineer ride on the narrow rear platform of the steamer of Engine Company No. 69. *Captain Clarence Meek*

Hey, Ma, They're Coming Down Our Street Hook & Ladder Co. No. 1 thunders down Olive Street in New Haven in about 1900. The boys think they can keep up with the horses. *New Haven Colony Historical Society*

Engine Company No. 32, Chicago This team of dappled grays hardly seems to be aware of the existence of a roadway, as the steamer races south on Michigan Avenue on September 14, 1908. *Chicago Historical Society*

Engine Company No. 80, F.D.N.Y. Pegasus had nothing on these flying steeds, which are almost completely airborne. Another picture of these magnificent animals appears on page 188. *Brown Brothers*

Deceptive Motion (above) Although the truck itself appears to be standing still, the well-matched horses prove otherwise. This fine white span is pulling Hook & Ladder Company No. 28 through New York streets in 1908. The apparatus is a seventy-five-foot Seagrave extension ladder, built in 1906. *Captain Clarence Meek*

Engine 80 on the Run (below) The three magnificent white steeds of this New York steamer are making fast time. The captain on the rear platform is ringing the bell. But in those days, people always *knew* when the engines were coming. *Ed. Waterman*

Ox-Drawn Fire Apparatus (above)
Speed was an important factor in getting equipment to the scene of a fire, but reliability was important, too, and in that respect these oxen could not be surpassed. Besides, this truck was very heavy to pull. And if the blaze seemed to be getting out of hand, someone always could walk ahead. *Fire Engineering*

Engine Company No. 2, Cleveland
(below) This steamer is making a fast run through the Public Square in Cleveland in 1910. The large canvas patch bearing the numeral "2" was sometimes used to keep burning coals from jumping from the firebox on a run over cobbled surfaces. *Western Reserve Historical Society*

Flying Horses   (above) This spectacular run of a Chicago steamer appears to be a drill, for there is no fire under the boiler. But if it *is* a drill, no one apparently informed the flying horses of that fact, for the animals seemingly believe that Mrs. O'Leary's cow's heifer has kicked over another lantern. *Chicago Museum of Science and Industry*

Fireboat Tender   (below) This is a fireboat tender of the Buffalo, New York, Fire Department. Instead of the standard 2½ inch or smaller hose carried for land companies, this wagon was equipped with 3½ inch lines for use by the larger pumps on Buffalo's fireboat, which was authorized in the 1880's. *Buffalo Historical Society*

Fast Time in Buffalo   This 3-horse hitch was attached to Engine Co. No. 30 of the Buffalo Fire Department, at South Park and Whitfield Streets. *Buffalo Historical Society*

Plenty of Smoke   (below) Steamers were available in several sizes, and the smaller types could be handled by two horses instead of three. Despite the hill, these steeds look quite fresh. *Fire Engineering*

The Last Alarm   This historic photograph
shows the last run of the New York Fire Department
with horses on December 20, 1922. The steamer be-
longs to Engine Co. No. 205. *Brown Brothers*

The Passing of the Horse

By the dawn of the twentieth century, the doom of the fire horse was apparent to the farsighted. But the successors of those firemen who had resisted the introduction of the animals were equally determined that the horses should not be supplanted by the machine age.

An article in *Scribner's Magazine* in 1902 declared that "it is highly probable that the days of the fire-horse are numbered." The author felt, however, that electricity would be the force that would unhorse the fire engine or, possibly, that steam would supply the propulsion power, although steam engines were too slow in starting to be a real threat to the horse.

In 1906, Wayne, Pennsylvania, acquired a gasoline-driven engine. In the following year, gasoline engines were simultaneously tried on fire apparatus in several communities. The New York Fire Department ordered its first motor equipment, a four-cylinder Knox-Springfield hose cart. But Alameda, California, purchased a complete gasoline pumper.

In the next few years, several steamers were converted into automobiles. This experiment was not successful, as the apparatus was too heavy for driving power in the rear wheels, directly beneath the ponderous boiler. The development of a front-drive motor, or tractor, proved to be highly successful: a completely self-contained two-wheeled engine was attached to old apparatus that had been designed for horses, and until well into the 1920's, the bulk of the nation's fire equipment was of this type. The gasoline-driven automobile that

One-Wheel Auto Horse   Tractors attached to equipment intended for horses by the St. Louis F.D.
Philip T. Nauman

Motorized Hook and Ladder A front-drive motor converted this old horse-drawn truck to the gasoline age. The tanks in front of the standing firemen are to raise the extension ladder. *Smithsonian Institute*

Strange Bedfellows This scene in Baltimore was photographed about 1912, when automotive equipment was beginning to encroach upon the domain of the horse. Gradually the encroachment became complete, but for a long time many firemen resisted the change as vehemently as their grandfathers had opposed the replacement of man power by horse power. *Peale Museum, Baltimore*

could use the same motor for both driving and pumping purposes was in service even prior to the introduction of the front-drive; but the latter had two big advantages: it could utilize the sturdy steamer which had an extensive remaining useful life and it could be dismounted for replacement by another tractor whenever the motor needed repairs (which was frequently in the early days).

The chronic breakdowns of the primitive gasoline engines were gleefully noted by the partisans of the horse. In 1912, the chief of the New York Fire Department wrote: "Again let me counsel caution in adopting motor apparatus too speedily. It is well to have in reserve at any rate a piece of horse-drawn apparatus to fall back on in case of any disarrangement of those employing newer motive power."

Horses were supplanted by a variety of mechanisms. First there were the self-propelled steamers; this was merely a revival of the mechanism that had been tried at various occasions since the intro-

duction of the first steamer, when the idea of a single steam plant to propel the apparatus and to work the pumps was conceived. There were various types of internal combustion engines, working on gasoline or kerosene or other fuel. There were electric-driven motors, with huge storage batteries supplying the current.

The public at large was slow to accept the change. The transition from horses to internal combustion engines was appalling not only to sentimental persons but to those with a sense of aesthetics. The early gasoline apparatus was grotesque. How could such ugly monstrosities take the place of the beautiful horses and the handsome old apparatus that had proven itself so frequently?

The machine, however, had heard that complaint before. The Industrial Revolution moved ahead inexorably.

Gasoline-driven engines worked for many years in the same department, and often in the same house, as the horse-drawn apparatus. Naturally

A Pioneer Gasoline-Driven Engine This self-propelled, gasoline-driven fire engine was delivered to Wayne, Pennsylvania, in 1906. It had a capacity of three hundred gallons per minute. *Waterous Company*

New York's First Gasoline Pumper This Waterous pumper was the first self-propelled gasoline engine delivered to the city of New York. The gasoline pumper had a capacity of nine hundred gallons per minute. *Waterous Company*

Ring Out the Old, Ring In the New
The exact moment when Engine Company No. 230 in New York lost its superb horses to the insensitive motor age in 1918. The new machines are about to be placed in the quarters just being left for the last time by the gallant steeds. The animal on the left is curiously regarding its replacement; the open-mouthed horse on the right is expressing itself in no uncertain voice; while the center horse merely stares ahead glumly. A moment later and this company's change from horse to gasoline power had taken place. Many regretted it. *Ed. Waterman*

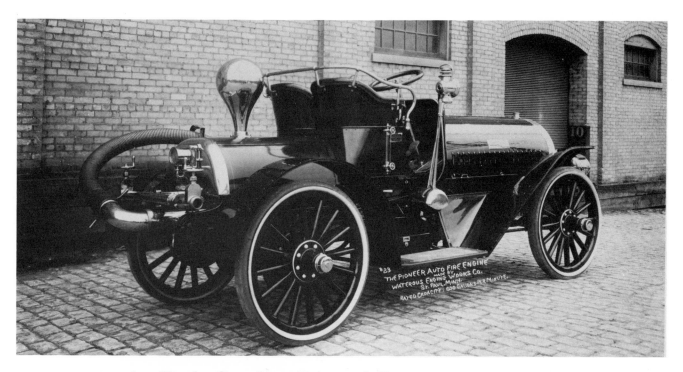

An Early Gasoline-Powered Pumper One of the first gasoline pumpers with its own propulsion plant. This engine was furnished to Alemeda, California, in 1907. The pumper had a capacity of six hundred gallons per minute. *Waterous Company*

The Christie Front Drive For more than twenty years, this type of motorized steamer was the workhorse of municipal fire departments. This Christie Front Drive was a complete power unit that occupied approximately the same position that the horses had had. The driver, as may be seen, was not obliged to waste his time with unnecessary gadgets such as gauges, meters, or dashboard controls. *Ed. Waterman*

New York's First Gasoline-Driven Pumper The New York Fire Department acquired this Nott-drive pumper for Engine Company No. 58 in 1911. Unlike virtually all of the later steamers, this was not tractor-driven; the propulsion was supplied by the rear wheels as in the standard automobile. This early model was not very successful. Note the size of the back wheels that had to be driven by the heavy chain. *Fire Engineering*

New Associates A horse-drawn steamer and an automobile steamer work side by side at this fire in New York City. Other equipment shows both types of propulsion power. Note how magnificently cared for the horses are. *Brown Brothers*

there were unofficial races on the way to fires. And when the horses got there first, there was considerable jubilation on the part of many firemen.

The replacement of a company's horses by a gasoline engine was generally a sad occasion. Most houses marked the occasion with a ceremony: the horses, decked with flowers or ribbons, would make one last "farewell" run, during the course of which the new automobile would be driven into the quarters that just had been vacated. The toughest, most cynical firemen were not ashamed to kiss their steeds at parting. Perhaps they *had* required a tremendous amount of care; maybe they *had* slowed down considerably. But the firemen had spent their entire professional lives with the horses. The animals were faithful, sympathetic, living comrades-in-arms. The new automobiles were still unproven rookies.

The New York Fire Department had more than fifteen hundred horses when the process of motorization was commenced at the end of the first decade of the twentieth century. The last run of this department with horses took place on Wednesday morning, December 20, 1922. Assistant Chief "Smokey Joe" Martin tapped in signal 5–93–205 from a firebox in front of Borough Hall in Brooklyn. The message "special-called" Engine Company No. 205 to Fire Box 93. In the quarters of that company on Pierrepont Street, automatic doors to the stalls clanked open, and five well-trained horses hurried to their places beneath harness suspended from the ceiling. Firemen snapped the collars and buckles of the three animals for the steamer and the two for the hose wagon; then, with a shriek from the steam whistle, the company dashed out. Penrose, Danny Beg, and Billy Griffin propelled the smoking steamer through the crowded streets of downtown Brooklyn, amidst throngs of Christmas shoppers, while, just to the rear, Waterboy and Bucknell sped along with the hose wagon. Straight to Box 93 raced the apparatus, but there was no fire. Only a shining new automobile pumper awaited their arrival. There were speeches by the fire commissioner and others; the company which had been the first one in the old City of Brooklyn to have horses was now to be the final company to be motorized. George Murray and John Foster, the drivers, said their sad good-bys to their mighty horses; so did Captain Leon Howard and all of the other firemen. Raymond McGill stepped into the new car and started the engine. Down another street were led the gallant steeds, their heads high. A few minutes later, in the quarters of 205 Engine, the company commander signaled to headquarters 4–4–4 205 ("We're back in service again"). But things were not the same. Old Jigs, the house fire dog, was disconsolate about his missing comrades. A veteran chief noted that "every old fireman lost at least one good friend when they were 'retired.'"

At about the same time, this melancholy event was being repeated in the other cities of the land. Honorably discharged, the remaining fire horses proudly stepped back into history. The end of an era had come.

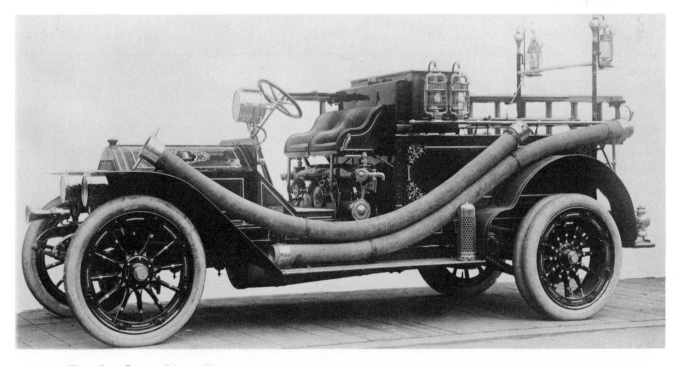

Early Gasoline Pumper   This gasoline-driven motor served both for driving and pumping purposes. It was built in 1910. *American-LaFrance-Foamite Corporation*

Fire Engines Today

American-LaFrance-Foamite Corporation

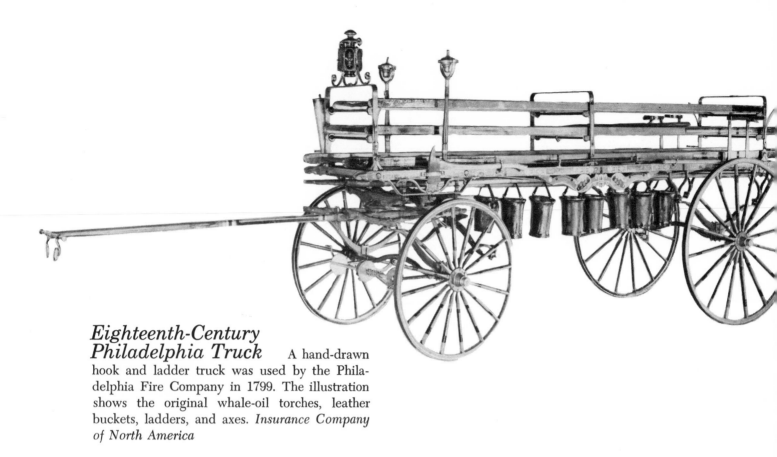

***Eighteenth-Century
Philadelphia Truck*** A hand-drawn
hook and ladder truck was used by the Philadelphia Fire Company in 1799. The illustration
shows the original whale-oil torches, leather
buckets, ladders, and axes. *Insurance Company
of North America*

Peter Pirsch & Sons Co.

The Seagrave Corporation

Gone is the gaily-painted "gooseneck" hand pumper. Some scrap heap has claimed the smoke-belching steamer. The hook and ladder truck that was drawn by mighty horses is now only a fading memory in the minds of middle-aged persons. The glamour peculiar to the old fire engines is a thing of the past.

But the fire apparatus of today has a fascination all its own. In an age that bows to the wonders of our new technology, fire engines are a shining example of human ingenuity and efficiency. The most sentimental oldster will excitedly turn from his workaday existence to ogle today's equipment.

The Age of Science is complicated, and so are the engines that must deal with its fires. Once the pumper and the hook and ladder truck were considered adequate for the job to be done. Today there are high-pressure spray trucks, rescue companies, searchlight cars, smoke ejectors, fire ambulances, airport crash units, chemical vehicles, mobile laboratories, double-ended tunnel engines. Apparatus is equipped with two-way radios, walkie-talkies, asbestos suits (for the "hot papas"),

gas masks, smoke helmets, acetylene torches, pneumatic drills, air compressors.

Fire fighting is partially mechanized today. Thermostats turn in alarms of fire when there is excessive heat. Smoke in a compartment may be automatically signaled to a control station. Sprinklers turn on their own water when the need arises.

But the age of push-button fire fighting has not arrived. Because of the hazards of today's technology, the fireman must be as courageous, as well trained, and as skillfully officered as he was in the past. Yet because his bravery cannot be improved upon, his physical equipment must be bettered to meet the growing demands of the time. And fire equipment has kept pace with the inventions and techniques of our age.

The apparatus as shown on the following pages may lack certain of the highly personalized characteristics of the old "masheens," even though today's engines are not strictly production-line jobs. But in this equipment one may see power, sturdiness, efficiency, and reliability. Such are the hallmarks of the Age of Science.

American-LaFrance-Foamite Corporation

American-LaFrance-Foamite Corporation

Mack Motor Truck Corporation

American-LaFrance-Foamite Corporation

The Seagrave Corporation

Ward La France Truck Corporation

The Hayes Aerial Ladder Fire Truck Company No. 2 of Richmond, Virginia, demonstrates with a Hayes aerial extension ladder in 1902. Hayes built the first turntable on a hook and ladder truck, in 1868. He had been a New York fireman before taking charge of the San Francisco Fire Department Repair Shop. *Valentine Museum, Richmond*

American-LaFrance-Foamite Corporation

207

Ward LaFrance Truck Corporation

Peter Pirsch & Sons Co.

The Seagrave Corp.

John Bean High Pressure Fog Firefighter